DO YOU KNOW . . .

- Where to find a writers' center that provides computers and copying machines, tips on publishing, and even job referrals?
- What techniques will make your essay for college admission or a grant shine among scores of other applicants?
- What you **do not** need to include on a job résumé?
- How a chart prepared beforehand can simplify the taking of minutes at a meeting?
- Why keeping a journal can develop your writing style—and expand your self-knowledge?
- How to overcome writer's block?
- Which computerized index accesses a thousand periodicals in seconds . . . what legal database lists nearly 800 legal publications . . . where you can find an on-line service that contains 300 databases . . . and how you can use all of them without leaving your home?

NO OTHER WRITING GUIDE IS AS COMPREHENSIVE AND UP-TO-DATE AS THE *21st Century Guide to Improving Your Writing*. IT PROVIDES EASY INSTRUCTION, DRILLS, AND PRACTICE THAT CAN LET YOU SEE A DIFFERENCE IN YOUR WRITING IMMEDIATELY—AND GIVE YOU THE COMPETITIVE EDGE WHENEVER YOU NEED TO USE THE WRITTEN WORD.

21st CENTURY GUIDE TO IMPROVING YOUR WRITING

21ST CENTURY

CENTURY

GUIDE TO

IMPROVING

YOUR WRITING

EDITED BY THE PRINCETON LANGUAGE INSTITUTE

DIANE L. ZAHLER, COMPILER

ELLEN LICHTENSTEIN, SPECIAL CONSULTANT

CLAUDIA H.C.Q. SORSBY, EDITOR

DANIEL C.A. HILLMAN, TECHNICAL CONSULTANT

Produced by the Philip Lief Group, Inc.

A LAUREL BOOK

Published by
Dell Publishing
a division of Bantam Doubleday Dell Publishing Group, Inc.
1540 Broadway
New York, NY 10036

Published by arrangement with The Philip Lief Group, Inc.
6 West 20th Street
New York, NY 10011

ISBN: 0-440-21727-X

Printed in the United States of America

Published simultaneously in Canada

June 1995

10   9   8   7   6   5   4   3   2   1

Contents

Introduction: Why Write?

Writing—does it seem old-fashioned to you? Everything nowadays is electronic. Telephones connect you with friends, family, business acquaintances. Modems hook you up to other people's computers. Books are quickly translated into movies or videos you can watch. And, literally speaking, you already know how to write. You can sign an order form, make out a grocery list, send e-mail to a friend. Why should you need a book on writing skills for the 21st century?

You need it because writing is becoming more important in this electronic age than ever before. Faxes can transmit letters and memos immediately, but you have to write them first. On-line services and e-mail can connect you and your computer to dozens, hundreds, or even thousands of people around the world, and they will know you through your writing.

This book focuses on *improving* your writing skills. There are two compelling reasons to improve your writing:

1. **Bad writing will keep you from achieving your goals.** Do you want to do well in school? Your research paper won't get an A if your punctuation is faulty and your organization is poor. Do you want a promotion at work? Your boss won't pay attention to memos that aren't coherently written. Do you want to publish your short story in *The New Yorker?* You don't have a chance if your sentences are awkward and your characters are undeveloped.

2. **Good writing will help you achieve your goals**. If you write well, you immediately have an advantage over others. In school, finely crafted essays get better grades. In business, well-written reports and letters earn respect. In the world of professional writing, thoughtful, cleverly organized, grace-fully written articles and stories are more likely to get published. And for day-to-day writing needs, highly developed writing skills lead to good communication.

With all the competition you'll face during your life—for grades, for higher salaries and promotions, for publishing contracts—you'll do far better if you write well. This book can help you with every aspect of your writing, from finding ideas for writing to developing and organizing your ideas to drafting, revising, and proofreading. It will take you through the basics of fiction and nonfiction writing, business writing, and personal writing. It can help you improve your word choice, sentences, and paragraphs. It will explain the rules of grammar, usage, and punctuation. It will give you pointers on using your computer for research and writing. Finally, it will tell you how to share your writing, through groups, organizations, and publishing outlets. You can learn to do all this by taking advantage of the most up-to-date electronic advances—databases, e-mail, and CD-ROM.

You can use the book in two ways. First, you can read it from start to finish, using its step-by-step techniques to improve each aspect of your writing. Or you can focus on the skills that you most need to improve. Are you uncertain about the rules of grammar? See Part II. Do you need help with your organization? Chapter 15 can help. Are your computer skills a little out of date? Check out Part V. However you choose to approach the book, one thing is certain: it can help you improve your writing.

Why write? Because in today's world, with computers, e-mail, and faxes, we are communicating more and more through writing. Why improve your writing skills? Because if you do, you will become a better communicator—and communication is what opens life's doors.

Diane Zahler

21st —
CENTURY
GUIDE TO
IMPROVING
YOUR WRITING

I

Types of Writing

1

Fiction

- *PLOT*
- *SETTING*
- *CHARACTER*
- *THEME*
- *MOOD*
- *FORMS OF FICTION*

When you write fiction, you are writing from your imagination. Sometimes your ideas may be based on fact, but the specific details that go into your work are your own creation. Many fiction writers use their own life experiences in their writing, while others venture far from reality. Of course, any work can combine categories. Virtually all fiction, however, includes the elements of plot, setting, character, theme, and mood.

PLOT

The **plot** of a fictional work is what the work is about. It consists of a series of events that tell a story. Usually a plot will start with an **exposition,** which introduces readers to the characters and setting. **Rising action** moves the plot along to a **climax,** in which the action comes to a dramatic high pitch. Next comes the **falling action,** in which the plot begins to draw to a close. The plot ends in a **resolution,** which determines the final outcome.

Often, the story will concern a **conflict** or **conflicts.** Conflict can pit a character against another character, or a character against another force, such as nature. Fiction can also feature **internal conflict,** in which characters experience conflict within themselves. You can introduce a conflict with a **narrative hook,** which is the point in your writing at which you present the problem, catching the reader's interest.

When you are considering plot:

DO make the exposition interesting while introducing your characters and setting. Many writers have difficulty in beginning their fictional pieces because they spend either too much or too little time introducing the plot. Your aim in writing an exposition is to tell exactly as much as your readers need to know to understand what will happen next—and no more.

DO develop a convincing resolution. You want to tie up all the loose ends, but you don't want to explain narratively exactly what happened. Let your characters and action do the talking for you.

DON'T make your resolution neat. It's all right to leave a few loose threads, as long as they aren't intrinsic to the plot. You don't want your reader to feel as though a Superior Being (you, the writer) has stepped in and cleaned everything up.

DO outline your plot by preparing a plot time line that shows when each event occurs. Various events might take place at the same time; a time line will clarify the sequence for you. The exposition, climax, and resolution should be clearly delineated.

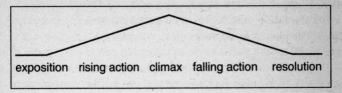

exposition   rising action   climax   falling action   resolution

Practice

1. Make a time-line outline for a fiction piece you know well or are reading at the moment. Show when the exposition, the climax, and the resolution occur, and include other important events.

2. Prepare a time-line outline for a plot of your own. Include the most important events, and show when the exposition, the climax, and the resolution occur.

SETTING

For some works of fiction, the **setting,** where and when the work takes place, is vitally important. For example, many science fiction tales are set far in the future, in claustrophobic spacecrafts or on distant planets. Settings such as these have a strong influence on the plot and characters.

The time frame of a story, novel, or play can make a huge difference in the language and the actions of the characters. Think about William Shakespeare's *Macbeth*. The author set the play in Scotland, some time before he was writing (the early seventeenth century). However, a contemporary movie version of the play, titled *Men of Respect*, retold the story in a modern setting. The characters spoke with New York accents, and instead of being Scottish nobility, they were mob-connected thugs.

When you are considering setting:

DO write about times and places you know or have researched. If your details are incorrect, there will surely be a reader who will know it.

DO make your setting an important part of your work. If you are writing a story set on a farm in the 1930s, be sure there is a reason for the time and place. Does part of your plot concern the Depression? Is your main character unhappy with farm life?

Practice

1. Think about possible settings for a story on each of the subjects below. Write a description of the setting you think would work best.
   a. a stowaway to the Far East
   b. an unexpected hurricane
   c. a gang confrontation
2. Consider one of these pairs of plays and/or movies. Each has been updated, with a corresponding change in setting. Explain how the change in setting influences the story.
   a. *Romeo and Juliet* → *West Side Story*
   b. *The Return of Martin Guerre* → *Somersby*
   c. *King Lear* → *Ran*

CHARACTER

The **characters,** or people in a work of fiction, are vitally important to its development. Their actions and conflicts move the plot along. As a writer, you can reveal your characters' **key traits,** or important aspects of personality, in two ways.

1. **Direct Characterization,** in which you tell your reader facts about your character.
2. **Indirect Characterization,** in which you reveal the character's traits in one of these ways:

   a. letting the reader know the character's words, thoughts, and feelings
   b. describing the character's looks
   c. revealing what other characters think and say about the character
   d. letting the reader see the character act

Here are examples of the two forms of characterization.

1. Direct Characterization:

   Stanton was a heavy child, and graceless. He lumbered rather than walked, and since he never looked where he was going, he often tripped and fell, his bulk landing on grass or concrete with a painful *thump*.

2. Indirect Characterization:

   "He oughta take charm classes," Mrs. Rabinowitz said, laughing. "That kid is such an oaf you wouldn't believe!"
   Stanton fled her laughter, but in his hurry to escape he tripped on the curb, landing in the street with a painful *thump*.

A character who is one-sided, only revealing one type of character trait, is called a **flat character.** Usually writers try to avoid flat characters in their writing, but sometimes you will find a one-sided character useful. You can use a flat character to point out other characters' traits or to advance the plot.

A character who is many-sided and who shows various traits is called a **round character.** Round characters are more interesting than flat characters because they are not entirely predictable. They are more like real people. You will want your **main character,** the person around whom much of the plot revolves, to be a round character.

Some characters change their personalities or attitudes over the course of a work. These are called **dynamic characters.** Other characters remain virtually the same. They are called **static characters.**

Keep in mind that you don't have to agree with your characters on every point. You don't even have to like them all. You will want them to be as much like real people as possible—and you certainly don't agree with or like everybody. If characters seem to develop wills and opinions of their own—good! It means that you're creating something believable.

When you're considering character:

DON'T stereotype. A clichéd character will be dull for the reader, who will know exactly what to expect from him or her. Beware the overprotective Jewish mother, the conservative midwesterner, the corrupt, baby-kissing politician. Your characters might possess these traits, as people in real life do, but that is not *all* they are made of. Give them unexpected personality twists, or make them act contradictorily. Your characters, or most of them, should be as three-dimensional as real people.

DO write a brief biography of one or more of your characters, or prepare a genealogy or family history. You can even sketch characters to get to know them better. The more you know about your characters, the easier it will be to present them convincingly.

Practice

1. Choose a character from a fictional work you have read recently. Prepare a family history for the character, even if the

information is not included in the work. Include details that help explain the character's personality traits.

2. Write a character sketch for a character of your own. Describe the character's physical traits, and tell what his or her personality is like.

THEME

The **theme** of a work of fiction is its central idea. The writer will rarely state the theme directly. Rather, the reader must read carefully to determine what the writer is saying about the subject. The subject and theme are different: the subject is what the work is about, but the theme is what the writer wants to communicate about the subject.

Not every literary work has a theme. Some are written purely for entertainment and don't try to convey a message of any sort. Most serious works, however, will have at least one theme. It is the theme that gives the work significance.

Usually, the theme of a literary work is a comment on human values or experiences. As a writer, you must decide what comment you wish to make about humanity as you think about your writing. Keep in mind that your whole work illustrates your theme. Every aspect of what you write is related to your theme—your characters, your setting, your plot, even the mood of your work. You will find that if you keep your theme in mind as you write, your writing will be more unified and coherent.

When you are considering theme:

DON'T use themes that have been used often before—unless you can think of a new, fascinating way to present them. You run the risk of having your reader compare your work to someone else's on the same theme—perhaps someone who has presented the theme better.

DON'T use your theme to preach or moralize. Though you can have a moral in mind, you want to leave it to your reader to discover it. Don't spell it out. You're writing fiction, not a sermon.

Practice

Think of a literary work you have read recently. Describe its main theme and explain how the plot and characters worked to illustrate the theme.

MOOD

The **mood** of a work of fiction, or its atmosphere, is the general feeling the work evokes. The writer's word choice, the plot's action, and the setting and characterization of a work all help create a particular mood. A story's mood can be somber, whimsical, cheerful, subdued, and so on. The mood of many Edgar Allen Poe stories, for example, is threatening and gloomy. On the other hand, the mood of *A Midsummer Night's Dream* is generally lighthearted.

When you are considering mood:

DO be sure your work's mood is consistent. That doesn't mean that the mood cannot change. In a longer work, the mood often does change many times. If the mood changes, however, you want to be sure there is a good reason for it.

DO create mood shifts that work dramatically and are appropriate. Mood shifts work especially well in horror, mystery, and suspense writing, where mood is very important to the plot. If you do create a mood shift, be sure it is well-planned and logical. It should have a dramatic purpose: Do you want to shock your reader? Do you want to reveal something unexpected about your character? Do you want to contrast two moods to make one seem all the stronger? Think of the scene in *Romeo and Juliet* in which Mercutio, fighting with Tybalt, is stabbed. The mood shifts suddenly from one of frenetic, joke-filled violence to one that is shockingly tragic. The shift serves to highlight the deadly side of the feud between the two families and to hint at the tragedy to come.

Practice

Try to recall a film you have seen recently that has a relatively consistent mood. Describe the mood, and give examples from the movie that support your interpretation.

FORMS OF FICTION

When you decide to write fiction, you can choose one of several **forms.** These include *novels, short stories, plays,* and *screenplays*. The form you pick depends on what you want to say and how you feel most comfortable saying it.

Short Story

A *short story* is a brief fictional narrative in prose. It is usually less than 25,000 words in length. When you write a short story, you will usually organize it around only one plot, which you must develop very carefully. Because the events in a short story are compressed due to its length, almost everything that happens will be important. You may wish to organize your ideas by making an outline. (See pages 175–177 for more information on outlining.)

Each character in a short story is also very important. There is not much time or space in which to develop characters, so you must carefully consider every clue to their personalities that you give your readers. You will probably not be able to include many secondary characters. Each of your characters should be linked somehow to the action of the plot.

A short story's theme is often crucial, since you don't have much writing with which to make an impact. You want your readers to remember what you have written because it says something meaningful about human existence. Be sure, however, that your theme doesn't overshadow your plot or characters.

The mood of a short story can be very important. Consider thoughtfully what sort of atmosphere you want to create within your story. Choose your words carefully to help develop that mood.

You will also want to consider point of view as you write your short story. (For more information on point of view, see pages 16 and 102–103.)

One of the best ways to learn how short stories can be organized is to read good examples of the genre. Some short story authors to read include Guy de Maupassant, Ernest Hemingway, Eudora Welty, Margaret Atwood, James Joyce, and Katherine Anne Porter.

Novel

A *novel* is a prose fiction work that is usually 50,000 words or more in length. Typically, a novel may include more than one plot, though a single plot is usually the main plot and other plots will be *subplots,* connected to the main plot but less important. The plot of a novel can unfold at a more leisurely pace than that of a short story, so as a writer you have more opportunity to include details in the rising and falling action. Be sure, when you write a novel, that you have resolved all your plots by the book's end.

Some fictional genres are more dependent on plot than others. In mystery and suspense novels, for example, the central question is usually "who done it"; characterization and setting are generally less important. Again, you may want to outline your main plot, particularly if you are writing in these genres. (See pages 175–177 for more information on outlining.)

Characterization in novels is also a more leisurely job than in short stories. You will probably develop several characters fully, and you will have the time and space to make them rounded and dynamic. Be sure that, if your characters change over the course of your novel, their changes are logical and are connected with the events of the plot.

In a novel you can include many settings if you want. A novel can take place over a period of time. Many family sagas encompass generations. The place in which you set your action can also change. Leo Tolstoy's novel *War and Peace,* for instance, has dozens of settings and spans decades, while James Joyce's *Ulysses* takes place in the city of Dublin over the course of a single day.

As the setting of a novel can change from scene to scene, so can its mood. You may need to convey various atmospheres at different points in your novel. Be sure that the mood reflects the characters' thoughts, feelings, and actions.

The theme of a novel is often what makes the work relevant to readers. Though the story may be set in a time and place foreign to readers, a universal theme will give it familiarity and meaning.

You will also want to consider point of view as you write your novel. (For more information on point of view, see pages 16 and 102–103.)

To see the many ways in which novels can be structured, you may want to look at the work of these novelists: Jane Austen, Henry James, James Joyce, John Steinbeck, Isabelle Allende, and Toni Morrison.

Play

A *play* is a dramatic fictional form. Like the short story and the novel, a play includes the elements of plot, character, setting, mood, and theme. However, plays are written to be performed by actors before an audience. This leads to differences in form and content.

The form, or *script,* of a play is usually divided into acts, and scenes within acts. The setting can change between scenes and acts, though it doesn't have to. The script begins with a list of characters, often with brief descriptions, and a description of the setting. It includes *stage directions,* which are instructions for the actors. It also includes *dialogue,* the words the characters speak. Characterization is given indirectly through dialogue and the actions of the characters, and depends greatly on the individual actor's interpretation of the part. Much of the plot is also revealed in dialogue, though stage directions help the actors know how the characters move.

The beginning of a play might look something like this:

THE WHITE OAK

CHARACTERS

JOE BOSWICK, a wealthy farmer
WILLA BOSWICK, BOSWICK's blind daughter
JULE, an itinerant sharecropper
TOM, the BOSWICK handyman

ACT I

Scene 1

[The Boswick living room. The furniture is dark and heavy, the atmosphere oppressive. WILLA sits in the darkened room knitting. Enter JULE, cap in hand. He stares at WILLA, and she raises her head, turning toward him. A moment of silence.]

WILLA: Is someone there?

JOE BOSWICK's voice from offstage: Willa? Is supper ready?

[JULE disappears, and WILLA springs up, obviously afraid.]

As you can see, the stage directions help describe the setting, provide the mood of the play, and give clues as to plot and characterization. They are written in brackets.

As a writer, you develop the theme of a play as you do with any other work of literature. The characters help illustrate the theme through their dialogue and actions. Some plays also have a narrator to explain events and move the story along.

You will find it useful to read and view plays so you can get ideas about structure and content—what works onstage and what doesn't. Some playwrights to keep in mind include William Shakespeare, Lorraine Hansbury, Lillian Hellman, Sam Shepard, and Athol Fugard.

Screenplay

A *screenplay* is a play that is written to be filmed. Like a short story, novel, or play, it has a plot, characters, setting, a theme, and mood.

You must construct the plot of a screenplay very carefully. It should not contain a lot of exposition; your viewers won't have the patience for long-winded explanations. As in a play, action and dialogue move the plot along. However, novelty in a screenplay is more important than in a play. Viewers usually see far more movies than they do plays, so they need new ideas and new twists on themes onscreen.

Characterization in a screenplay, as in a play, depends heavily on the actor playing each part. As a screenwriter, you want to be sure you have developed your characters completely and made them realistic and believable. However, you also want to leave room for the individual interpretation of the actor. What you end up seeing onscreen or onstage may not be much like what you visualized when you wrote the character; that's a common problem for both screenwriters and playwrights.

Unlike other forms of fiction, a screenplay includes camera directions. Because you can direct the camera action, you can show the audience exactly what you want it to see. Here are some camera terms you may use in a screenplay.

POV—this means point of view, and indicates a scene seen through the point of view of something or someone specific.

CLOSE-UP—a shot that shows a detail.

PAN—a shot where the camera moves without stopping.

CLOSE, MEDIUM, LONG SHOT—indicates the camera's distance from a scene.

ZOOM—camera moves in on the subject.

TILT SHOT—camera tilts down or up.

AERIAL SHOT—shot taken from a plane.

FREEZE FRAME—camera holds still.

MONTAGE—a sequence of camera shots.

DISSOLVE—a time lapse shot where one shot disappears into another shot.

CUT—a shot ends suddenly and another begins.

FADE IN or OUT—picture comes up from blackness or fades into blackness.

Because a screenplay often relies more on images than words, you have a certain freedom that you do not get with other fictional forms.

A page from a screenplay might look like this:

INT   KITCHEN   DAY

CAROL and NORM wash dishes silently, obviously angry. Suddenly NORM drops a plate, which smashes on the floor. TILT SHOT to plate on floor.

CAROL

You did it again; there's another one gone. What's wrong with you, anyway?

NORM

(bending down to pick up pieces)

Wrong with *me?* It's you who's as knotted up as old fishing line. Look, if you don't want Kate to stay here, why don't you just say so?

Although the writer has described the basic shot, he or she has still left many decisions up to the director and the actors. More than any other form of fiction, a screenplay is a collaboration— among writer, director, actors, photographers, set designers, and so on. (It may also become a collaboration among writers, since movie studios are notorious for demanding many re-writes, often by different writers.) When you write a screenplay, you are writing a fluid work that can be realized in many differ-ent ways.

To acquaint yourself with the form and the different methods of constructing a screenplay, you may want to read some of the following: *Citizen Kane, Rear Window, Nashville,* and *2001: A Space Odyssey*.

Fiction is a mode of writing that gives you great freedom to stretch your imagination. Whether you choose to write short stories, novels, plays, or screenplays, you can make your work distinct and memorable by paying careful attention to plot, character, setting, theme, and mood.

2

Nonfiction

- *RESEARCH*
- *NOTETAKING*
- *DOCUMENTATION*
- *FORMS OF NONFICTION*

When you write nonfiction, you are writing about something that is true and is based on fact. You can use nonfiction to describe someone or something, to persuade readers of something, to narrate or tell a true story, or to explain. When you write nonfiction, you want to be accurate, clear, and detailed.

RESEARCH

When you do research for a nonfiction work, you look into the facts you need to write about your subject. There are several useful ways to do research, and you can combine them effectively or use just one.

One of the most useful research tools you have is the *library*. The library contains fiction, nonfiction, and reference books, periodical materials, and nonprint materials that can help you in your research.

One of the major guides to finding what you need in a library is the *catalog;* it lists that library's holdings. If the library is connected to others, such as in a large university system, the catalog will list the system's holdings. Catalogs used to be done in card form, but most libraries have now transferred them to computers (some still keep the actual cards, too). Computerized catalogs provide the same information as card catalogs, but they display the information on a computer screen. Some computerized catalogs can give even more information, such as whether or not the book you want has been checked out. (See Part V, chapter 19, for more details about computerized catalogs in libraries.)

Each book in the library is represented in the catalog by an entry (or card), and there are at least three entries for each book: author, title, and subject. They are arranged alphabetically. Author entries list the name of a book's author, last name first, and also include the book's title. Title entries list the title first. Subject entries list the book's main subject, and include author and title. They are particularly useful if you need several books on the same subject.

The catalog tells you the location of each book. Fiction is usually arranged alphabetically by the author's last name, and biography and autobiography are arranged by the subject's last name. Nonfiction and reference works are given call numbers that tell you where in the library they are located. Some libraries arrange their nonfiction by using the Dewey Decimal system, which arranges books by numbers in ten main categories. Other libraries use the Library of Congress system, which arranges books by letters in twenty-one main categories.

Here are three sample catalog entries—for author, title, and subject.

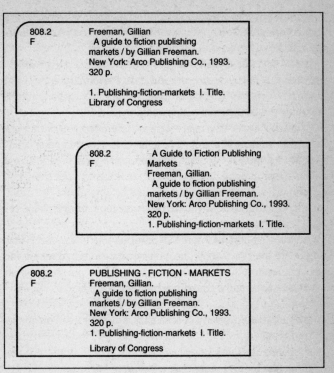

Another research guide that you may find useful is the *Reader's Guide to Periodical Literature*. The *Reader's Guide* lists the authors, titles, and subjects of articles in most major periodicals. A new volume of the *Guide* is published each year. Each listing in the *Guide* includes the name of the magazine, the date, and the pages on which the article is found. Some libraries have the *Guide* on computer. It's easier to use on computer because all the listings by a particular author or on a particular subject are grouped together.

Once you have located the article you need, you can look at the periodical if your library carries it. Even if they don't, your librarian may be able to get it for you through inter-library loan, or at least tell you where you can find it. Some periodicals are kept in miniature form, on microfilm or microfiche. Your librarian can show you how to use these.

Other periodical guides include *The New York Times Index*, the *Social Sciences Index*, the *Business Periodicals Index*, and the *Education Index*. Each of these includes an explanation of how to use it in the front of the book.

Libraries also carry many general reference works that are helpful in starting research. These include general and specialized encyclopedias, general and specialized dictionaries, and collective or general biographies. If you look up your topic in a general reference work, you will often be able to use the information you find to help you narrow your topic or determine related topics of interest.

Another important source of information is the *interview*. When you interview someone, you ask questions and record the answers, in note form, on tape, or both. When you conduct an interview, keep these guidelines in mind:

1. Be sure that your subject is an expert on the topic you are researching.
2. Prepare your questions ahead of time. Try to think of questions that require more than a yes or no answer.
3. Be sure to get your subject's permission to record or take notes on the interview and to use the interview in your writing.
4. Try to make your subject feel at ease. A comfortable, relaxed, and prepared interview style will lead to a more candid and open interview.

Include your subject's name, position, and the date and place of the interview at the start of your tape or of your notes.

Practice

Pick one of these topics. Use the catalog at your local library to locate three books on your topic. Write down the authors' names, titles, and locations of your books.

1. computer graphics
2. the Hundred Years' War
3. apartheid
4. Euripides
5. triathalons

NOTETAKING

When you begin your research, you will want to have a computer, a notebook, or a series of 3 x 5- or 4 x 6-inch notecards for notetaking purposes. It's essential to take accurate, detailed notes. They will help you to:

1. collect useful and correct information
2. keep track of your information
3. prepare your bibliography (see pages 28–30)
4. avoid plagiarism (see page 25)

Start by writing down the bibliographic information for the source you are using. Include the title, the names of the authors and/or the editors, the place of publication, the name of the publishing company, and the date of publication. If your source is a periodical, include the volume number (if necessary) and the title of the article as well as the periodical title.

In your notes, you can do several different things. You can write a *summary,* or a summing up, of important information. A summary is shorter than the material from which it is taken. It includes the main points of the original, but only the most important of the details. You can also *paraphrase,* or restate the original information in your own words. A paraphrase is usually about the same length as the original. Finally, you can write down a *quotation.* A quotation is word for word the same as you found it in your source. You must enclose a quotation within quotation marks. (For more information on quotations and quotation marks, see pages 26, 135–136, and 133–135.)

Write the page number or numbers of the book or article at the top of each page or card of your notes. A sample might look like this:

> Jacobson, Trudi. *State of the Art Fact Finding.* NY: Dell Publishing Co., 1993.

> CD-ROM—means **Compact Disk-Read Only Memory.** Can only read data from disk—no writing on it. Requires CD-ROM player to access. Some encyclopedias stored on it. Has space for 275,000 pages. (page 29)

Try to keep your notes organized. Keep notes from a given source on the same page or card, or in one file; if you're taking a lot of notes, number the pages or cards. Also, use your notes as a place to write down new questions to pursue as they come up. When you have taken all the notes you need, you will have control over the information that will best help you in your writing.

Practice

Refer back to the Practice on page 23. Look in one of the books you located, and take at least a page, or three notecards' worth of notes on the topic.

DOCUMENTATION

When you use other people's ideas or words in your writing, as you often will when writing nonfiction, you must **document** your source. If you don't, you are committing intellectual theft, because you are stealing someone else's ideas and misrepresenting them as your own: this is called *plagiarism*. Plagiarism is against the law, and in many situations you can actually be prosecuted for it. In the academic community in particular, plagiarism is considered to be an extremely serious offense. If you plagiarize as a student, you risk disciplinary action, an automatic failure, and even suspension or expulsion. If you knowingly plagiarize as a professor or teacher, you will jeopardize your professional credibility.

You should document your sources in two ways. The first way is to refer to your source in the body of your writing. You can use a *parenthetical reference,* you can use *endnotes,* or you can use *footnotes.* Usually, writers use parenthetical references; sometimes, however, the type of writing you are doing or the audience for whom you are writing will require you to use endnotes or footnotes.

Parenthetical documentation is a reference in parentheses within the body of your paper. It refers to a work in your bibliography. Follow these rules for parenthetical documentation:

1. If you refer to a work with one author, write the author's last name and the page number on which you found the information.

   (Workford 58)

2. If you refer to a work with more than one author, include all the authors' last names, or write the first author's last name and the words "et al."

   (Workford, Hoskins, and Turner 79); (Workford et al. 79)

3. If you refer to more than one work with the same author, include the title or a shortened title in your reference.

(Workford, *Beautiful Samoa* 124)

You place your parenthetical reference directly after the information you are using, and before any punctuation.

The islands of Samoa make up one of the most exotic places in the world. Filled with strange animals seen nowhere else, overflowing with tropical plants, Samoa is often considered the ultimate destination for the adventurous tourist (Wilson 230).

If you refer to the author's name in the paragraph, you need only include the page number of the reference in parentheses.

As Wilson points out, even an increase in tourism has not blighted the natural beauty of these jungle islands—yet (104).

If you are using a short quotation, you should place the parenthetical reference after the final quotation marks and before the final punctuation.

The intrepid adventurer on Samoa will quickly find that the abundance of flora and fauna is "unequaled anywhere else in the world" (Wilson 96).

A long quotation, over three lines, is written without quotation marks and indented uniformly. It includes the parenthetical reference at the end, after the final punctuation.

Western Samoa is still closely linked with long-ago Polynesia, but American Samoa is strongly stamped with the modern world. Pago-Pago, the capital, is beset with traffic jams and modern social ills. Western Samoa, on the other hand, is a poverty-stricken nation, but here you can still see history. (Wilson 252)

You may sometimes find it necessary to use endnotes or footnotes. Endnotes are placed at the end of a paper or book, before the bibliography. Footnotes appear at the bottom of the page on which the reference occurs.

Both footnotes and endnotes are indicated by superscript numbers after the text to which they refer and after punctuation that is part of a quotation.

> Samoa has been examined by scientists and poets alike. Margaret Mead performed her famous studies of native adolescent life here[8], and Robert Louis Stevenson lived for a few years and "died on his own Treasure Island."[9]

When you write the first footnote or endnote for a particular work, include the following source information:

1. number of the note
2. author's name, first name first, and any additional authors' names
3. title of the article and publication or of the book
4. publication information: place and company if a book, and date
5. numbers of the pages from which the information is taken

[3]Martin Stringer, "Wonders of Borneo," *National Geographic,* Sept. 1993, p. 64.

Later references to the work need only include the note number, the author's name, and the page numbers.

[6]Stringer, pp. 67-68.

The main difference between footnote and endnotes is their placement. Endnotes used to be considered easier to include, because you could simply list them in order on a separate page, with the heading **Notes** at the top, after the body of your work. For footnotes, you had to estimate the amount of space needed at the bottom of each page. Today, most word processing programs include a footnoting function, which not only adjusts the page space automatically but also keeps the numbering of the notes in order. This makes the choice of which to use one of personal taste; some readers find it irritating to have long footnotes at the bottom of every page, while others find it irritating to continually flip back to the end of the material. If you have a great many notes which are content-oriented, as well as bibliographic, you may choose to use both styles. The substantive material can appear as footnotes, while the bibliographic references can be listed at the back as endnotes.

In nonfiction writing for which you have done research, you should also include a *bibliography*. All the books that gave you substantial information should be included in your bibliography. A bibliography is arranged alphabetically by authors' last names. Each entry should include the following information:

Book:

1. name of author(s) or editor(s)
2. title
3. series and volume numbers, if any
4. edition, if not the first
5. publication information: city, name of publisher, date of publication

Charma, Devendra, and Moss, William. *Satan and Milton.* Boston: Cambridge University Press, 1992.

Article:

1. name of author(s)
2. title of article
3. title of periodical
4. volume number and/or date
5. pages of the article

Floris, Kallie. "Women on the Bench." *Newsweek,* 9 May 1993, pp. 42-46.

Here are some additional rules for bibliographies.

If you include more than one work by an author or authors, use a 3-em dash (————) in place of the name after the first entry, and arrange the works by date.

Stark, Merry. *Juvenile Diabetes*. NY: Hammond Press, 1990.
————. *Controlling Your Diabetes*. NY: Hammond Press, 1993.

If a book is put together by an association and does not have an author, treat the name of the association as if it were the author's name.

American Library Association. *Multicultural Children's Books*. NY: ALA Press, 1994.

If an article is from a journal with a number, use a colon between the journal number and the page numbers.

Margaux, Kitty. "Lyme Disease and Your Dog." *Journal of Veterinary Medicine* 64: 37-39.

If you include an article from a newspaper, write the information as follows: author, headline, name of paper, date, section, page number, and column number.

Williams, Anthony. "Park Crime Takes a New Twist." *Newsday*, 11 May 1994, Sec. 2, p. 14, col. 2.

If you include an interview, note the name of the person interviewed, the word "Interview," and the date.

Morris, Mark. Interview. 24 March 1992.

It is important to be consistent in your bibliography. If you write "Lynn Messing, ed." in one entry, don't write "Donald Griggs, editor" in another.
Remember, too, to include in your bibliography all of the

works you have cited in your text. Your readers should easily be able to locate and identify all the sources of your information.

Practice

Write a bibliographic entry for the source you used to take notes on page 24.

FORMS OF NONFICTION

There are several forms of nonfiction that you may find yourself writing. One of the most common is the *expository essay*. An expository essay is a work of prose nonfiction that does one of several things: it describes, it persuades, it narrates, or it analyzes.

In a descriptive essay, you are telling about a person, place, thing, feeling, or situation. You want to appeal to your reader's senses of sight, smell, touch, hearing, and taste to create a mental picture. As in certain types of fiction writing, you can use *figurative language*—similes, metaphors, and personification—to help create a picture (see page 104 for more information on figurative language).

Some descriptive essays take the form of magazine articles on travel, science, art and architecture, music, dance, and many other subjects. If you want to look at examples of descriptive essays, you might read collections by Peter Matthieson or Lewis Thomas.

A persuasive essay tries to get the reader to share your opinion. When you are preparing to write a persuasive essay, you need to consider what point you will be making and how you will support that point. You will want to support your opinion with facts, examples, and quotations to make the strongest argument possible. (See pages 99–100 for more information on persuasive writing.) A newspaper or magazine editorial is often a type of persuasive essay. If you want to read some examples of persuasive essays, look at collections by William F. Buckley or Anna Quindlen.

When you write a narrative essay, you are telling a true story. A narrative essay can be a simple account of events that happened, or it can be an interpretation of the events and their significance. It is important to keep the sequence of events clear in a narrative essay, so your readers can understand what has happened.

Histories and many autobiographies and biographies are written in narrative essay form. Personal narratives and anecdotes are often narrative essays as well. You might want to try reading narrative essays by Erma Bombeck, Joan Didion, or Norman Mailer.

An analytic essay is perhaps the most difficult kind of essay to write. When you analyze, you are looking at a subject critically and seeing how it works, whether the subject is a motorcycle or a work of literature. Analysis takes a whole and separates it into its parts. Then it investigates the parts, either to see how one or more works or to see how they relate to the whole. If, for example, you analyze a literary work, you will focus on one or all of its parts: character, plot, setting, theme, point of view, or language. You can ask yourself the following questions about the work. With the answers, you will be able to formulate an analysis.

1. What is the basic plot of the work?
2. Who are the main characters? Are they flat or round?
3. What conflicts do the characters face?
4. What is the narrative point of view of the work?
5. How does the plot affect the work?

6. What is the setting of the work? Is it vital to the work? Why?
7. Does the work include figurative language? If so, what function does it serve?
8. Does the work include irony—that is, a difference between what is expected and what occurs or what is said and what is meant?
9. Does the work include symbols—people, places, or things that have meaning beyond their physical existence?

Once you have found the answers to these questions, you can focus more carefully on one aspect of the work to analyze. If you are analyzing something other than a work of literature, your questioning can follow the same general lines:

1. What facts do I know about my subject?
2. What do I need to know about my subject?
3. What causes and effects does my subject have?
4. What importance does my subject have?

When you have found an aspect of the subject to analyze, use facts, examples, and quotations to support your analysis.

If you are in the process of applying to a college, university, or other type of program, you will probably have to write an *application essay*. College application essays are essentially autobiographical in nature. They are subtly persuasive—you are trying to persuade the college to accept you as a student. They may be narrative, descriptive, or analytical. The focus of your essay will depend largely on the question you must answer, which could range from the vague—"Tell us about yourself"—to the specific—"What is your favorite book? Explain how it has influenced you."

The trouble with application essays is that hundreds or even thousands of other students are applying at the same time you are. Some of them will probably try to impress the admissions officers with extras such as videotapes or other attention-grabbing devices. While these devices might impress some officers, they are more likely to groan and say, "Oh no. Not another senior playing Hamlet!" Your best bet is to make your writing stand out. That means treading a fine line between the unusual and the silly or shocking. You can surprise an admissions officer with the following approaches:

1. the humorous approach
2. the unexpected topic
3. the unusual form

Choose only one of these approaches. Remember, the application question might limit your possibilities. If, for example, the question asks for an essay about your take on the plight of the homeless, your topic has been chosen. You'd probably be unwise to approach it humorously. Instead, choose an unusual form—an imagined or real interview with a homeless person, for example, or a description of your night at a homeless shelter.

Be sure, as you're writing, that you reveal something of yourself in your work. The application essay is not part of a writing contest; it is part of an admissions contest. You want the person reading it to understand why you are a better applicant than the dozens of others whose work he or she read that day. That means showing something unique about yourself to your reader.

After you've completed your college essay, have someone whose opinion you trust read it to be sure you've struck the right balance. Remember to doublecheck any facts you have included. Spend extra time revising and proofreading (see Part IV, chapters 17 and 18, and Part V, chapter 23). Keep in mind that the application essay is often the only clue to your individuality an admissions officer has.

Another form of nonfiction you may write, especially if you are in school, is the *research report*. This is a report based on facts that you have found by researching and then synthesized.

When you choose a topic for a research report, you should ask yourself several questions. First, is the topic of interest to you? You will find your research much more interesting and challenging if you are fascinated by your subject. Next, is the topic broad enough to fill a paper but narrow enough to focus on? You want to be sure that you'll have enough to write about, but not so much that your report loses focus. Finally, is there enough information available on the subject? You won't know this for sure until you begin your research.

Once you have found a topic of the right size that interests you, you will research it in one or more of the ways described at the start of this chapter. You'll take notes on your research and document your sources. Often when you write a research paper, you will find it useful to make an outline. (See pages 175–177 for more information on outlining.)

All research involves finding the answers to questions. As you write your paper, you will want to make sure your original questions have been answered. If other questions come up during your research that are important to understanding your topic, try to answer them as well. Use all the research tools you can to find information, and be sure the tools you use are up-to-date, reliable, and authoritative. Support your thesis with facts, reasons, and examples.

Another common type of nonfiction writing is the *news article.* News articles are structured to answer five basic questions: *Who? What? When? Where?* and *Why?* Most newspaper articles will try to answer these questions—or at least the first four—in the first paragraph.

The most important part of a newspaper article is the *lead,* or the first few sentences. The lead must be strong enough to make the reader sit up and take notice, while still giving the important information about the event. Here are two leads for the same news story. Which do you think is stronger? Why?

> At eleven o'clock last night in Wilmington Park, two ten-year-olds attacked and stabbed a twelve-year-old to death and stole his mountain bike.

> A twelve-year-old boy was stabbed to death in Wilmington Park late last night. Two neighborhood ten-year-olds did the killing. Why? They wanted his mountain bike.

Two elements are crucial to good news writing.

1. Solid research. Your facts give your readers new and interesting information; accuracy is essential.
2. Clear, concise writing. Use active verbs and strong descriptive words.

There is a major difference between the straight news story, which answers the basic five questions and does little else, and the news feature, which relies more heavily on its lead and on descriptive details. The first is a rather dry, factual account of what happened. It is the basis for news reporting. Keep in mind that newspapers often cut stories at the last minute, for example, to provide space for a late-breaking story. Editors will generally cut from the end of the piece, which is another reason why the main information needs to go up front.

The feature is what, for many of today's readers, makes the news interesting. It offers the human interest side of the story, and often gives more detailed information. It may focus more on the *why* of the story than on the other questions.

A feature story can be narrated in the first person, using "I" as the filter for the events. It can include humorous anecdotes that help illustrate what occurred or who was involved. Quotations are often important in a feature. They add color and interest to a subject that might otherwise be dry. However, when you use quotations in a news story, you must be especially careful. Follow these rules:

1. Don't use quotations out of context.
2. Quote your subject in full, or, if you delete part of the quote, don't change the meaning of the words.
3. Doublecheck your quotation. If you have the words on tape, listen again. If you're unsure of a quotation, check back with your source. Misquoting leaves you open to a lawsuit.

A *magazine article* starts where the newspaper article leaves off. When you write a magazine article you provide your reader with the facts. Then you tell your reader what to do with the facts—be sympathetic, take action, feel glad, form an opinion.

Your style as a writer is more important in a magazine article than in a newspaper article. You are creating something closer to a short story. It has a beginning, a middle, and an end. If it is well done, it will keep your reader interested in what happens next.

A magazine article can have many purposes and take many forms. You can write to inform, to entertain, or to persuade. Your article can be a personal narrative, a description, or a short biography. All magazine articles should contain the following, however:

1. A strong lead. Your opening draws your readers in.
2. A sensible structure. You can arrange your article in any of these ways:

   chronologically
   categorically
   listing
   question and answer
   comparison and contrast
   cause and effect

You can also combine structures. However, you must be sure your writing is well organized and consistent. (For more information on organizing writing, see pages 175–178.)

3. A strong conclusion. You want your readers to remember your ending, just as you wanted them to be interested in your lead.

Here are some ways to create strong leads.

1. Begin with a vivid description. This draws your readers into the world of your story.
2. Write a humorous anecdote. This sets your readers up to be entertained.
3. Use a quotation. This introduces your readers to an expert on your topic.
4. Use an unusual fact. This grabs your readers' interest.
5. Start with a strong opinion. This tells your readers what to think.
6. Start with a question. This encourages your readers to find an answer.

There are many situations in which you might find you have to write a *speech*. Perhaps you've been nominated for an award— or a close relative has. Perhaps you're the best man at a wedding, or you're the guest of honor at a banquet. Speech writing has much in common with other types of nonfiction writing, but it has a few rules of its own.

A speechwriter has to consider the audience, first and foremost. A speech on civic responsibility given to a group of fifth graders will differ greatly from a speech on the same subject addressing the city council. Your audience will help determine your tone and your word choice. (For more information on audience, see pages 99–101.)

When you have your speech topic, whether you've chosen it yourself or had it assigned to you, you'll want to research it as you would any other topic. Take notes as for a report. Even though no one but you may ever read the speech, your notes will provide the foundation for it. Prepare an outline. (For more information on outlining, see pages 175–177.)

Here are some rules that will help you make your speech more effective and resonant.

1. Use parallelism.

   nonparallel: We must look to the future. Then we can gather our strength and forge ahead.
   parallel: We must look to the future; we must gather our strength; we must forge ahead.

2. Use repetition. Remember Martin Luther King, Jr.'s famous "I Have a Dream" speech? He repeated the words "I have a dream" over and over—and they made a tremendous impact.
3. Use anecdotes. When appropriate, a humorous story that illustrates a point will keep the audience's attention.
4. Use facts and statistics. Numbers indicate authority to an audience.
5. Use simple words. Unless your audience is a panel of experts or Nobel Prize winners, jargon and long words will go over their heads.

When your speech is ready, practice it. First, time your reading. Then slow down and read it again (many people rush when speaking in public). Read it into a tape recorder and play it back. The more familiar you are with your words, the better prepared you are, the less likely you'll be to draw a complete blank when it's time to deliver them.

You've learned the basics of writing nonfiction—how to use the library and interviews for research purposes, and how to take notes and document sources. You're aware of the main considerations in writing essays, speeches, and articles. Remember that in nonfiction writing, clarity, organization, and accuracy are vital. And *always* credit your sources!

3

Business Writing

- *RÉSUMÉS*
- *LETTERS*
- *MEMOS*
- *MINUTES*
- *REPORTS*

When you write for business purposes, it is important that you write well. You want to communicate your ideas clearly and concisely, and you want to make a good impression on the associates who read your work.

RÉSUMÉS

One of the first types of business writing you will ever do is the **résumé**. A résumé is a general summary of your qualifications. It is usually divided into three parts:

1. personal information
2. education
3. work history

In the section on personal information, you need to list your full name, your address, and your telephone number. List your fax number too, if you have one, and your e-mail address. Any other information is optional, and possibly detrimental to your objective. Potential employers do not need to know your age, your height and weight, or your marital status (and it is illegal for them to ask, by the way).

If you are a first-time job seeker or sending out a general application that is not aimed at a particular position, you can include a statement titled "Career Objective." Otherwise, you should address your career objective in your cover letter. Your next heading can either be "Education" or "Work History," depending on which one you want to emphasize. If you are a recent graduate and your only past job was at Burger King, you'll want to stress your education. If, however, you left school twenty years ago and have an impressive job history, you'll want your work to stand out.

When you detail your education, list your most recent degree first. If you were involved in courses or school activities related to the position you want, mention that. List any awards or honors you have achieved. If, however, you did not graduate from college, you may wish to eliminate this section.

Under work history, list your most recent job first, with the dates of employment and the address of the workplace. If your résumé will fill more than a page, you may choose to leave out those jobs that don't relate to the position you are seeking. One rule of thumb is that you can add a page to your résumé for every ten years of experience you have (since school). Write a *very* brief description of your duties in each job. Include any business affiliations you have, such as organizations or clubs to which you belong. List professional writing you have done or courses you have given. End your résumé by writing "References Available Upon Request."

The organization of your résumé is, to some extent, up to you. You will want it to look professional and attractive, to stand out without looking too obvious. It is a good idea to print it with a letter-quality printer or to have it professionally printed. Most personnel managers recommend using paper in the white to cream range with black type.

See the sample résumé below:

Eleanor R. Stevens
112-72 Natchez Parkway
New Orleans, LA 70603
504-555-0792

Work Experience

1990–present
Pastry Chef, L'Ambiance Restaurant, 1212 North Avenue, New Orleans, LA 70603. Supervise six assistant chefs. Responsible for all desserts.

1984–1990
Assistant pastry chef, Cajun Cafe, 14 West 14th Street, New York, NY 10014. Created dessert menu.

1982–1984
Baker, Soho Bakery, 240 West Street, New York, NY 10003. Made breads, pastries, cakes.

Professional Organizations

1991–present
Member, American Association of Pastry Chefs.

Publications

Puff Pastry Perfection, McDougall Publishers, 20 West 21 Street, New York, NY 10023, 1992.
Cake, Cake, Cake, McDougall Publishers, 20 West 21 Street, New York, NY 10023, 1990.

Awards

1991
Winner, Puff Pastry Competition, Wichita Falls, KS.

1990
   Runner-up, Betty Crocker Bakeoff.

Education

1982
   Culinary Institute of America, Poughkeepsie, NY. Graduated with high honors.

1980
   Cornell University, Ithaca, NY. Graduated from the School of Hotel Administration.

References Available Upon Request.

Practice

Prepare your résumé. Experiment with listing your experience in different orders and forms. Try to come up with a résumé that gives you a professional profile and will stand out in a crowd.

LETTERS

There are many types of business letters you will write during your work life. Most of them will follow the same basic format, which includes these parts:

1. your address—at the top
2. the date—below your address
3. inside address—name, title, company, and address of the person to whom you are writing
4. greeting—"Dear" followed by a colon or comma
5. body—the text of the letter
6. closing—usually "Sincerely" or "Very truly yours," followed by a comma

7. signature—your signature, with your name and title (if you have one) typed below

Usually a business letter is written in block form; that is, paragraphs are not indented and are separated by double spacing.

The first kind of business letter you will probably write is the *cover letter,* or letter of application. This accompanies your résumé when you apply for jobs. If possible, you should address it to a specific person. You can call the personnel division of a company to ask for the name of the appropriate recipient. Your cover letter should explain why you are writing—are you responding to an ad? Have you spoken to someone in the company? It should tell why you think you are right for a particular position at that particular company. Here is an example of a cover letter:

4004 Commish Road
Groton, NY 13068
January 14, 199-

Mr. Paul Fremont
Personnel Director
Traveller's Magazine
104 West Street
Los Angeles, CA 90049

Dear Mr. Fremont:

As you requested on the telephone this afternoon, I am sending you a résumé listing my qualifications for the position of staff travel writer. A mutual friend, Megan Ober, suggested I apply for the job, and when she told me it was at *Traveller's,* I called you immediately.

I have always been an enthusiastic reader of *Traveller's,* and have followed your travel articles both as an armchair voyager and as an actual traveler. As you can see on my résumé, I have worked abroad in London and Tokyo, and have traveled extensively in Europe and the Far East. I used those opportunities to pen travel articles as a freelancer, which have been published in various magazines.

My experience as a travel writer, my familiarity with the computer system used at *Traveller's,* and my love of travel lead me to think that I might fit in well at your magazine. I hope you agree, and I look forward to hearing from you. Thank you for your consideration.

Sincerely,

Marilyn McDaniels

This letter addresses a particular person, explains the writer's relationship with the organization, stresses her familiarity with the field, and points out her qualifications for the job.

Much of your business correspondence will be routine. The standard formula for routine business letters includes the following rules:

1. Refer to correspondence or communication received.
2. Answer all questions and give complete information.
3. Thank the addressee for interest or business.

Here is a sample of a routine business letter:

Acme Refrigerators, Inc.
145 Oceanside Avenue, San Diego, CA 90032

June 1, 199-

Ms. Marisol Ruiz
Kentucky Chicken Huts, Inc.
9992 Los Vidas Boulevard
Tempe, AZ 85282

Dear Ms. Ruiz:

Thank you for your letter of May 12 inquiring about prices and availability of our refrigeration units. We would be pleased to supply Kentucky Chicken Huts with the 300 units you requested, at a discount price of $650 per unit. Shipping and handling would add another $45 per unit and would take approximately three weeks.

Thank you for your interest in Acme. Please address any further questions to me at 213-555-2212. I look forward to hearing from you further about your order.

Very truly yours,

Judy Davis
Vice-President, Acme

Other possible forms of business letters you may need to write include:

1. order letters
2. complaint letters
3. letters of resignation

When you write an *order letter,* you want to be sure you include all the information necessary to process your order. This includes:

1. a description of the merchandise, including the name or catalog number of the item, its size and/or color, the number required, and the price per item;
2. an indication of the method of shipment you want;
3. an indication of the method of payment you intend;
4. instructions on speed of delivery, if any.

A *letter of complaint* must be specific, too, but its tone is more important than that of most business letters. Try to keep the tone matter-of-fact and objective, even if you are annoyed or frustrated at the situation. Include the following information:

1. the reason for your complaint;
2. your requirements for an adjustment.

A *letter of resignation* is an important letter in your business career. Whether you are resigning because you've changed careers, because you've found a better job in the same business, or because you simply hate your job and can't work there anymore, your letter should express appreciation for your association with the company and regret at your leaving. Remember, you are likely to come across the people you work with later in your career. You want to leave them with pleasant feelings about you; you also want to be able to get a recommendation from them, if necessary. You may *need* their help later on. A letter of resignation should include the following:

1. the date your resignation becomes official;
2. the reasons for your resignation;
3. an expression of appreciation for the company;
4. an expression of regret over leaving the company.

In most business letters, you'll find it advantageous to keep your language simple and your tone businesslike and positive. Avoid using the passive voice in business letters. (For more information on the passive voice, see pages 67 and 115.)

When you prepare an envelope for a business letter, address it in this way:

your name
your company name
street number and name
city, state, and zip code

                                        addressee's name
                                        position, if known
                                        company name
                                        street number and name
                                        city, state, and zip code

Practice

Write a business letter of complaint to a firm whose merchandise or business practices have disappointed you in some way, or to a government office or official. Follow the rules for business letters.

MEMOS

The business **memo** is a method of communication within a company. A letter is usually too formal under the circumstances, so you use an interoffice memo with a less formal tone instead. A memo is usually organized with these headings in the top left, each followed by a colon.

Date:
To:
From:
Subject:

Your memos will usually have one of these purposes:

1. to give instructions
2. to address a problem
3. to give information

When you write a memo to give instructions, you should be as clear as possible. You will usually organize instructions using time, or chronological, order. (For more information on chronological order, see pages 92 and 177.) Clarify your instructions by including time-order words such as *first, next, then, finally,* and *last.*

When you write a memo to *address a problem,* begin by stating the problem clearly and concisely. Analyze the reasons for the problem. Then suggest a solution or solutions to the problem. Support your solution with facts, statistics, and examples.

When you write a memo to *give information,* keep your purpose in mind. It might help to prepare an outline of the information you will give. Don't include unimportant or unrelated details; they will detract from what you are saying.

Here is a sample memo that addresses a problem.

Date: February 27, 199-
To: Jake Stiles, Mailroom Supervisor
From: Ramona Wells, Manager
Subject: Duplicate names

Please note that we have two employees with the same name, Richard Wilson. These men have been receiving each other's mail since January, when the second Wilson was hired.

Keep in mind that the Wilsons work in different departments on different floors and have different middle names and nicknames. Richard Thomas Wilson (Rick) works in Promotion on the third floor. Richard Lanford Wilson (Dick) works in Shipping on the first floor. If these differences are not enough to identify whose mail is whose, please send a mail clerk with the questionable letters so the employees can make the decision themselves.

Thank you for your attention to this matter.

Practice

Compose a memo that gives step-by-step instructions for a familiar procedure. Break the steps down carefully. Make the memo simple and concise enough to be understood by everyone in the company for which you work.

MINUTES

When you attend a business meeting, someone will probably take notes, or **minutes,** on what occurs. That someone could be you. Taking minutes can be an important and difficult job: important because your minutes are the only official record of what went on in the meeting, and difficult because the meeting will not stop or even slow down to let you organize your writing.

Your best bet when taking minutes is to begin the meeting well organized. If your meetings are attended by many people, free-flowing, and confusing, you might want to prepare a chart beforehand. A sample chart might have headings such as the following:

Meeting Date:

Time Begun: Time Ended:

Attending:

Information Given   Suggestions Made   Responses   Decisions

Be sure to identify the speaker who offered each piece of information, suggestion, and response.

The final format of your minutes will probably follow the lines of previous meeting minutes. Look over a copy of your company's minutes well in advance of your first meeting. If you have suggestions for improving the form, bring them to your supervisor.

REPORTS

In many different businesses, you will be asked to prepare and present **reports**. In many ways, a business report is similar to a research report. You research information for it, you take notes, you prepare an outline, and you document your sources. (For more information on research reports, see page 34.) However, there are two parts to a business report that do not usually appear in a research report: a *summary,* at the beginning of the report, and an *appendix,* at the end of the report.

The summary says very briefly what your report says at length. It states your purpose, your problem, and your conclusions. You should write your summary after finishing your report. Only then will you know the full scale of your research and be able to sum up your conclusions. The summary is useful for those associates who do not have the time or inclination to read your entire report but still want to know what it contains.

Your appendix follows your bibliography. It contains material that you need to support your conclusion, such as graphs, charts, surveys, photographs, maps, tables, and so on. You may refer to these items in the body of your report, but since they are grouped together at the end, your readers will not look at them if they do not have to. If a graph, chart, or map is absolutely intrinsic to understanding the content of your report, you should include it in the text. If it simply helps to support your conclusions or to clarify your information, include it in the appendix.

You've learned the basics of business writing. During your working career, you will probably encounter and use variations on these standard formats. The most important things to remember about any business writing are: be brief, be simple, be accurate.

4

Personal Writing

- *JOURNALS*
- *PERSONAL LETTERS*

When you use a form of personal writing, your main purpose is to express yourself. The journal you keep, the letters you send—these often say more about how you really feel and who you really are than any other writing you will do. Your personal writing can also serve as the basis for other kinds of writing. It can be a gold mine of ideas. It can also be a way for you to practice writing. Just like any other skill, writing is improved through practice. The more you write—and the more you read of others' writing—the better your own writing will be.

JOURNALS

Through the ages, writers and other people have kept **journals,** or diaries. A journal is a place where a person can reveal himself or herself without fear of discovery. Your journal doesn't have to be the simple recitation of daily events that it might have been when you were ten years old. Instead of just writing down what happened to you, you can use the day's occurrences to explore. How did the events make you feel? How can you describe them in a new way?

Don't just use your journal to record what happens. Write down ideas you have for future writing projects. Describe someone you see whom you think might make an interesting character in a story or play. Note a news story you hear on television that might be useful at work. Jot down the title of a book or film that gets an interesting review on the radio.

Here are two important rules for journal writing.

1. Be honest. There's no point to keeping a journal if you're not telling the truth. The reason for your journal is to explore your thoughts and feelings, but you can't do that until you're willing to write them down.
2. Be spontaneous. Write when you want to write. Don't struggle over form or style. Write "stream of consciousness" if you want—your thoughts exactly as they emerge from your mind.

Once you are used to writing in a journal, you can begin to experiment with it. Try doing the following with your journal:

1. Include drawings, poems, and songs—your own, if you feel inspired, or things you see, hear, or read that move you. Explain how they make you feel, and why.
2. Write about yourself in the third person—as "he" or "she." This allows you to distance yourself from yourself. If you think of yourself as a character, you'll gain a whole new perspective on your life.
3. Write dialogues. They can be real or imagined, with others or with aspects of yourself. Use these dialogues to explore your feelings about events or about other people.
4. Include a character sketch of someone about whom you have written in your journal. An in-depth description can

help you to understand both the person and your own
thoughts and feelings about him or her.
5. Describe your dreams. You can learn a lot about yourself by
   investigating the reasons for and meanings of dreams. You
   can also use dreams as a springboard for other writing.
6. Use your journal to record positive feelings as well as negative feelings. It's easy to fall into a pattern of expressing only
   anger, pain, or envy in a journal, because these are emotions
   that are often not accepted in social situations. Express them
   in your journal, but try writing about happiness, excitement,
   and joy as well. Touch both sides of your personality.

All of these techniques can help you expand your self-
knowledge. They can also aid in developing your writing style.
Writing in your journal will open you up to writing freely and
unself-consciously. From there, it is only a step further to writing a short story, essay, or article.

Practice

Begin keeping a journal. Use a notebook or computer to
record your experiences, thoughts, and feelings. Try to write in
your journal on a daily basis.

PERSONAL LETTERS

A letter to a friend can be another way for you to explore the
boundaries of your feelings and of your writing style. Many famous writers, such as Gustave Flaubert and Flannery O'Connor, have had collections of their correspondence published.
These letters reveal much about the writers' personal lives, and
show how their writing changed and matured over the years.
Writing letters also gives you a practical way to practice

writing. You are maintaining communication with a friend or relative at the same time that you are trying out new words, ideas, and styles.

The form of a personal letter is somewhat different from that of a business letter. It includes a heading—your address and the date. It does not have an inside address, however. Your salutation should be followed by a comma, and the body of the letter should consist of indented paragraphs. The closing is usually informal—anything from "Best wishes" to "Love" will do, and below that goes your signature.

Here is an example of a friendly letter:

> 249 Beacon Street
> Boston, MA 02101
> April 30, 199-

Dear Phil,

   I'm writing this on the plane; we just said good-bye at the airport, but I feel like our conversation's still going on. It was so good to see you! It's funny, but I half-expected you to be the same pesky little cousin I used to torment during all those endless family reunions. Now you're about to enter law school!

   Listen, take advantage of my invitation to use the lake cottage. It's only used in July and the first half of August; if you want it during June or at the end of the summer, feel free. You could also use it during the year if you need a retreat from school for a while. Let me know when I'll be seeing you next.

> Love,
> Louise

The envelope for a personal letter is addressed the same way as a business envelope, except it does not include titles or company names.

You can write personal letters for many purposes: to communicate, to entertain, to describe, to persuade. Creative letters can be short stories or essays. You can write a movie review to tell a friend what you thought of a new film, or a short play to describe a highly dramatic family gathering. A letter helps you to keep in touch with friends and relatives in a way that a telephone call can't do. You can't reread—or replay—a phone call, and it's a rare phone call that allows you to create a mental picture of what the caller is describing. Above all, a letter lets you express yourself through writing. You can tell your thoughts and feelings, and you can experiment with your writing style.

If you write on a computer, you may find it useful to keep your letters on disk. That way, you can keep track of whom you've written to and what you've said. You can also note how your writing has changed over time. If you don't use a computer, you can photocopy your correspondence and file it for the same purposes.

E-mail is the newest form of personal letter. When you send e-mail to someone, it is usually a note or letter composed on computer, and sent via a modem or computer network directly to someone else's machine. The recipient can read on screen or print it out. Many people are finding e-mail to be a quick and easy way to communicate. Since it is so easy and quick to send, it also tends to be quite casual and informal.

There are a few types of personal letters in which you won't have much freedom of expression. These include:

1. thank-you notes
2. R.S.V.P.s
3. condolence notes

When you write a **thank-you note**, you are responding to an occasion or a gift. Include the following in your note:

1. Refer to the occasion or gift.
2. Tell what the occasion or gift meant to you.
3. Thank the giver.

When you write an **R.S.V.P.** (short for the French phrase "Respondez-vous, s'il vous plait," or "Please respond"), you are answering an invitation. Include the following in your response:

1. Refer to the event to which you have been invited.
2. Accept or decline the invitation.
3. If you decline, and if it is appropriate, give a reason.

When you write a **condolence note**, you are expressing sorrow over a death. Condolence notes can be the hardest type of letter to write. It is difficult to know what to say in the face of death; everything you think of will probably sound clichéd. In a condolence note, however, what you say is not as important as the fact that you've said it. The bereaved will be grateful for your sympathies even if they have a greeting-card sentiment. When you write a condolence note, keep these pointers in mind:

1. Express your sympathy. Don't make statements such as "I know how you must feel." However, if you have recently and similarly been bereaved, you might point out some thought or action that helped you through your experience.
2. If appropriate, include a memory of the deceased that illustrates how he or she affected you positively.
3. Offer to help—*if* you mean it. A statement such as "If there is anything I can do to help, just call me" is only clichéd if it is not sincere.

Practice

Write a personal letter to a friend or relative. Try to use your letter as an opportunity to improve your writing skills as well as a method of communication. Pay attention, too, to the form of your letter.

Personal writing in all its forms— from journals to personal letters, and any other writing you do to express yourself—can help you grow and change as a writer. It gives you the chance to experiment with style and form, and it allows you to understand yourself better, which helps to free you to write as you want to write.

II

Grammar and Usage

5

Parts of Speech

- *NOUNS*
- *VERBS*
- *MODIFIERS*
- *PRONOUNS*
- *PREPOSITIONS*
- *CONJUNCTIONS*
- *VERBALS*
- *APPOSITIVES*

Every time you speak or write, you are using parts of speech—nouns, verbs, adjectives, and so on. You're probably using most of them the right way, but there are many rules to remember. Knowing the rules makes it easier for you to write well and easier to communicate with others.

NOUNS

A **noun** is a word that names a person, place, thing, or idea.

person: The **artist** experimented with new techniques.
place: The **forest** was dark and silent.

thing: The **wheel** spun wildly.
idea: Tamar was filled with **happiness.**

A *common noun* is a general word for a person, place, thing, or idea. A *proper noun* names a specific person, place, thing, or idea. Proper nouns are capitalized.

common: The **ballplayer** hit a home run.
proper: **Babe Ruth** hit a home run.

A *concrete noun* names something that can be recognized by the senses. An *abstract noun* names something that can't be seen, heard, touched, tasted, or smelled.

concrete: The **manager** gave a speech.
abstract: The song was full of **sorrow**.

A *compound noun* contains more than one word. Some compound nouns are hyphenated. Others are written as one word or two words. Check a dictionary if you are not sure how to write a compound noun.

The **flight engineer** studied her landing **checklist** before adjusting the **radio-transceiver**.

A *collective noun* names a group.

The **flock** of geese flew south.

A *possessive noun* shows ownership or possession. You can make most nouns possessive by adding an apostrophe and *s*. Make plural nouns that end in *s* possessive by adding just an apostrophe.

Rita's book
the **children's** video games
the **judges'** opinions

Forming Plurals

You can make most nouns plural by adding *s*.

chair → chairs

Make some nouns that end in *o* plural by adding *es*.

echo → echoes

Make nouns that end in *s*, *x*, *sh*, or *ch* plural by adding *es*.

gas → gases   box → boxes
rash → rashes   itch → itches

Make nouns that end in a consonant and *y* plural by changing the *y* to *i* and adding *es*.

butterfly → butterflies

Make many nouns that end in *f* or *fe* plural by changing the *f* to *v* and adding *es* or *s*.

loaf → loaves life → lives

Some plurals are formed in an unusual way.

mouse → mice   woman → women
foot → feet   ox → oxen

Some plural nouns are the same as the singular noun.

elk   sheep   deer

Practice

Find each noun in this paragraph. Identify each as common or proper, concrete or abstract, singular, plural, or collective. State whether each is compound or possessive.

As Carrie O'Donnell entered the restaurant, the maitre d' rushed forward to seat her. He escorted her to a table, which was laid with a lace tablecloth and fresh flowers. Elegance was evident throughout the dining room. It was the perfect setting for an important business lunch.

VERBS

A **verb** is a word that names an action, a condition, or a state of being.

An *action verb* describes physical or mental action.

Jasper **wrote** an article for publication.
She **considered** several possibilities.

A *linking verb* connects the two parts of a sentence—the subject and the predicate. The *subject* is the part of the sentence about which something is said. The *predicate* tells something about the subject. (For more information on subjects and predicates, see Chapter 6.) The most common linking verb is *be*. The forms of be include **am, is, are, was, and were.** Other common linking verbs are **look, seem, grow, appear, become, smell, and feel.**

The driver **was** ready.
The air **smelled** oily.

A *helping verb* is a verb that goes with another verb. Common helping verbs include **am, is, are, was, were, has, had, have, will, do, does, did, can, could, may, might,** and **must.**

The police officer **had thought** the parade was over.
The president **could speak** to the group.

Sometimes helping verbs are separated from main verbs.

The contestant **could** not **guess** the answer.
Has Julia **hired** a replacement?

Verbs can be one of two *voices:* **active** or **passive.** If a verb is **active,** the subject performs the action. If a verb is **passive,** the subject is acted upon, or receives the action.

active: I shot the dog.
passive: The dog was shot.

Every verb has three tenses: the **present tense,** the **past tense,** and the **future tense.** The tense you use tells when the action you are describing takes place. To form the past tense of most verbs, add **d** or **ed.** To form the future tense of most verbs, include the helping verb **will.**

present: The swimmer **turns** expertly.
past: She **kicked** hard.
future: She **will reach** the finish line first.

Other verb forms include the *present participle* and the *past participle.* To form most present participles, use the helping verb *be* and add *ing* to the verb. To form most past participles, use the helping verb *have* and add *d* or *ed* to the verb.

present participle: The professor **is explaining** the experiment.
past participle: We **have tried** to follow his instructions.

Irregular verbs follow different rules. To determine how to form the past tense and past participle of irregular verbs, you must memorize them or look them up. You probably know most of these and use them correctly without even realizing it, but many people still trip up occasionally. Some irregular verbs have the same verb form for the past tense and the past participle.

past tense: Joan **lost** the race.
past participle: She **has lost** races before.

Other irregular verbs form the past participle by adding *n* or *en* to the verb.

past tense:	The thief **stole** the wallet.
past participle:	He **has stolen** my credit cards.

Still other irregular verbs change a vowel from *i* (present tense) to *a* (past tense) to *u* (past participle).

present tense:	The final bell **rings**.
past tense:	The bell **rang** loudly.
past participle:	The last bell **has rung**.

Finally, some irregular past participles are similar to the present tense of the verb.

present tense:	Juan **goes** on vacation today.
past tense:	He **went** to San Martin last year.
past participle:	He **has gone** there for five years.

Here are some other common irregular verb forms.

PRESENT TENSE	PAST TENSE	PAST PARTICIPLE (with HAVE)
wear	wore	worn
take	took	taken
put	put	put
teach	taught	taught
bring	brought	brought
sit	sat	sat
choose	chose	chosen
speak	spoke	spoken
swim	swam	swum
begin	began	begun
sing	sang	sung
do	did	done
eat	ate	eaten
give	gave	given
know	knew	known
write	wrote	written
see	saw	seen

Practice

1. Identify each of the underlined verbs in these sentences as an action verb, a linking verb, or a helping verb, and whether it is in the active or passive voice.

    a. The writer **finished** her manuscript.
    b. She **was** glad to be done.
    c. Her agent **had waited** for weeks to see it.
    d. He **wants** to send it to an editor.
    e. Will the book **be published** by the editor?

2. Rewrite this paragraph. Change the underlined present tense verbs to past tense. Change the underlined present participles to past participles.

    For some people, trains <u>are</u> the best way to travel. Passengers <u>sit</u> in comfortable seats and <u>see</u> the world pass outside the window. These travelers <u>are taking</u> their time. They <u>eat</u> delicious meals and <u>speak</u> to fellow passengers. Each passenger <u>is putting</u> comfort ahead of speed.

MODIFIERS

A **modifier** is a word that tells about other words. There are several types of modifiers.

An **adjective** is a modifier that describes a noun. Adjectives can tell **what kind, how many** or **how much,** or **which one.** They are especially useful in descriptions and in poetry.

what kind: Carmen bought a **red** car.
how many: She already has **two** convertibles.
which one: She drives **that** car.

An **article** is a kind of adjective. *Definite articles* include **the, this, those,** and **that**. They describe a particular noun. *In-*

definite articles include **a** and **an**. They do not describe particular nouns.

definite article: Please show me **the** printer.
indefinite article: Do you see **a** salesperson?

A *proper adjective* is formed from a proper noun. Always capitalize a proper adjective.

We decided to see a **German** film.

You can choose to use more than one adjective to describe a single noun. You can also place your adjectives in various parts of the sentence.

The **enormous, elegant** yacht sailed into the harbor.
The crew, **young** and **tanned**, guided it expertly.

An *adverb* is a modifier that describes a verb, an adjective, or another adverb.

describes a verb: The dancers performed **energetically.**

describes an adjective: They were **very** graceful.
describes an adverb: The dance ended **too** quickly.

Adverbs tell **how, when, where,** and **to what extent.**

how: Ms. Vrebeck works **hard.**
when: She files reports **weekly.**
where: She works **downtown.**
to what extent: She **never** misses a deadline.

Many adverbs are formed by adding *ly* to an adjective.

calm   →   calmly   silent   →   silently

Adverbs can be placed in various parts of a sentence. The placement of an adverb can change the sentence's emphasis.

Wildly, the crowd applauded. (emphasis on the crowd's wildness)

The crowd applauded **wildly.** (emphasis on the crowd's applause)

Adjectives and adverbs can be used to compare. Most one-syllable adjectives use *er* to compare two nouns and *est* to compare more than two nouns. Most adjectives of more than one syllable use *more* to compare two nouns and *most* to compare more than two nouns.

Yesterday was **hotter** than today.
Tomorrow will be the **hottest** day of all.
The humidity was **more uncomfortable** today than yesterday.
It is **most uncomfortable** just before a storm.

Adverbs can compare actions in the same way.

This office manager words **harder** than the last one.
The **hardest** worker is the summer intern.
He types **more quickly** than I do.
Gerry types the **most quickly** of all of us.

Some adjectives and adverbs have different forms for comparison.

ADJECTIVES

good	better	best
bad	worse	worst

ADVERBS

well	better	best
little	less	least
much	more	most

PRONOUNS

A **pronoun** is a word that takes the place of a noun. The noun replaced by a pronoun is called its **antecedent.**

antecedent: **Christopher Columbus** is a controversial figure.
pronoun: Was **he** a hero or an oppressor?

The following are *personal pronouns.*

I	he	she	we	they	you
me	him	her	us	them	it

A *possessive pronoun* is a pronoun that shows ownership. **My, mine, your, yours, their, theirs, his, her, hers,** and **its** are possessive pronouns.

This seat is **mine.**
That woman says it is **her** seat.

A *reflexive pronoun* is one to which *self* or *selves* is added. Reflexive pronouns can be used either to reflect action on the subject or to emphasize a noun or pronoun.

The actor threw **himself** into the role.
No one was more surprised than the actor **himself.**

Demonstrative pronouns include the words **this, that, these,** and **those.**

This is an excellent antique store.
That is a really beautiful quilt.

An *indefinite pronoun* does not usually have an antecedent. The following are indefinite pronouns.

all	most
anyone	much
anything	neither

anybody	nobody
anything	none
both	noone
each	one
either	several
everybody	some
everyone	somebody
everything	someone
many	something

An *interrogative pronoun* is used to ask a question. Interrogative pronouns include **who, whom, which, what,** and **whose.**

Who left the meeting early?
What was the outcome of the vote?

Practice

Circle the pronouns in this paragraph. Identify the type of pronoun. For each pronoun that has an antecedent, draw an arrow pointing back to the antecedent.

The set was in an uproar. It was hot, crowded, and noisy. No one seemed to be in charge. Finally, the director took over. She ordered the actors to ready themselves. The makeup artists finished their touch-ups and rushed away. Everybody grew quiet. This was the moment of truth.

PREPOSITIONS

A **preposition** is a word that shows how a noun or pronoun is related to another word in a sentence. Common prepositions include:

about	above	according to
across	after	against

along	among	around
as	at	because of
before	behind	below
beneath	beside	between
beyond	by	down
due to	during	except
for	from	in
inside	into	in place of
instead of	like	near
next to	of	off
on	onto	on top of
out	out of	outside
over	regarding	since
through	to	toward
under	underneath	until
up	upon	with
without		

The *object of a preposition* is the word the preposition links with the noun.

The lights went out **during** the storm.

During is the preposition; **storm** is the object of the preposition.

A *prepositional phrase* is a preposition, the object of the preposition, and any modifiers of the object.

Before the concert, the musicians were nervous.
They forgot their fears **after the music started.**

Prepositional phrases can be used as adjectives or adverbs. They can modify nouns or verbs.

adjective: The seats **near the stage** are
                                the best.

adverb:	The concert started **at night-fall.**
adjective and adverb:	The roar **of the crowd** echoed **beyond the concert arena.**

Practice

Underline each prepositional phrase. Tell whether each phrase acts as an adjective or an adverb.

The dancer spun across the stage. Her partner lifted her above his head. The audience beside the stage gasped. They could see that something had gone wrong with the lift. In an instant, the dancers had collapsed in a heap.

CONJUNCTIONS

A **conjunction** is a word that connects words, phrases, and clauses. (For more information about clauses, see Chapter 6.) *Coordinating conjunctions* join words, phrases, or clauses that are equivalent. They include the words **and, or, but, nor, for, yet,** and **so.**

Mars **and** Ares were names for the same god.
Ares was his Greek name, **but** Mars was his Roman name.
He was the god of war, **so** soldiers prayed to him before battle.

Correlative conjunctions are used in pairs. They include **either-or, neither-nor, both-and, not only-but also,** and **whether-or**.

The subway car was jammed with **both** businesspeople **and** schoolchildren.
Either someone would have to get off, **or** the doors would never close.

A *subordinating conjunction* begins certain clauses. Some common subordinating conjunctions include the following:

after	although	as	because	before
if	once	since	so	than
though	unless	until	when	where
whether	while			

Although the meeting had gone on for hours, the board had not reached a decision.

Practice

Underline the conjunction in each sentence. Tell whether it is a correlative, coordinating, or subordinating conjunction.

1. The critics and the people liked the movie.
2. It was neither a remake of a French film nor a dull action adventure.
3. Although it had big-name stars, the film was fresh and innovative.
4. Both the known actors and the unknowns were very good in it.
5. The screenwriter and the director were nominated for Academy Awards, but the actors were passed over.

VERBALS

A **verbal** is a word formed from a verb. However, you use verbals as other parts of speech.

A *gerund* is a verb form that ends in *ing*. You use a gerund as a noun.

Many people have taken up **racewalking** as a form of exercise.

A *gerund phrase* includes the gerund and its modifiers. You use the whole phrase as a noun.

Getting to class on time was nearly impossible for Jan.

A *participle* is a verb form that you use as an adjective. (You can refresh your memory on how to form past and present participles by looking back at pages 00–00.)

present participle: Shana had a party for the **visiting** professor.
past participle: The **tired** woman had to meet and greet all the guests.

A *participial phrase* is a participle and its modifiers. You use the whole phrase as an adjective.

The horse **pawing the ground** is expected to be the next Derby winner.

An *infinitive* is a verb form that begins with *to*.

Herb wanted **to write**.
He sent his stories **to be** read by editors.
He studied **to be** a writer.

An *infinitive phrase* includes an infinitive and its modifiers.

To understand the tax laws is a major accomplishment.
Most people are pleased **to get a refund.**
Some people do their own taxes **to save money.**

Practice

Identify each underlined verbal phrase as a gerund phrase, a participial phrase, or an infinitive phrase.

1. The skaters were *competing in the Olympics*.
2. They practiced hard *to prepare for the finals*.
3. Every day found them *skating for hours*.

4. The skaters, *filled with enthusiasm,* performed some wonderful moves.
5. *Applauding wildly,* the audience helped them *to win the gold medal.*

APPOSITIVES

An **appositive** is a word or group of words that renames a noun.

The lecturer, **a geneticist**, spoke at length.

An *appositive phrase* includes the appositive and its modifiers.

The audience, **science students from the college**, listened raptly.
A speaker of great renown, he kept them on the edge of their seats.

Practice

Combine these pairs of sentences by making the second sentence into an appositive phrase.

1. Harry Houdini was popular around the turn of the century.
   He was a well-known magician.
2. Houdini could free himself from a ton of concrete submerged in a river.
   He was a great escape artist.
3. Houdini died after being punched in the solar plexus.
   The solar plexus is an area at the bottom of the stomach.

This chapter explored how to use nouns, verbs, modifiers, pronouns, prepositions, conjunctions, verbals, and appositives.

You can use this knowledge to write sentences that are grammatically correct and to correct sentences that misuse grammar. By acquainting yourself with the rules of grammar, you make sure that you can be understood in whatever medium you choose to express yourself.

6

Parts of a Sentence

- *KINDS OF SENTENCES*
- *SUBJECTS AND PREDICATES*
- *COMPLEMENTS*
- *CLAUSES*
- *SENTENCE TYPES*

Now that you've learned—or refreshed your memory of—the rules of grammar, you can use those rules to build grammatically correct sentences. If we use building a house as a metaphor for writing, the parts of speech are the mortar that hold the sentences, the bricks of the structure, together.

KINDS OF SENTENCES

A **sentence** is a word group that expresses a complete thought. There are four basic kinds of sentences. A *declarative sentence* makes a statement and ends with a period. An *interrogative sentence* asks a question and ends with a question mark. An *imperative sentence* commands and usually ends with a period, or occasionally an exclamation point. An *exclamatory* *sentence* shows strong feeling and ends with an exclamation point.

declarative:	The secret of a good soufflé is in the egg whites.
interrogative:	Are your egg beaters really clean?
imperative:	Be sure the oven isn't opened as it bakes.
exclamatory:	Oh no, the soufflé fell!

Practice

Identify each of these sentences as declarative, interrogative, imperative, or exclamatory.

1. Do you think news shows have grown more exploitative?
2. They always show the same sort of stories.
3. Some reporters are shameless!
4. How can we protest?
5. Just turn off the television.

SUBJECTS AND PREDICATES

A sentence is made up of two parts. The **subject** of a sentence is the part about which something is said. The *simple subject* is the word or group of words that acts, is described, or is acted upon.

The window dresser hurried to complete the Christmas windows.

The *complete subject* consists of the simple subject and its modifiers.

The window dresser's expert hands worked quickly.

The **predicate** of a sentence tells what the subject is experiencing or what is being done to the subject. The *simple predicate* is only the verb.

The passers-by **watched.**

The *complete predicate* includes all the words that tell about the subject.

They **saw the window become a wonderland.**

Subjects and predicates can be compound.

compound subject: **Shoppers and workers** stopped to gaze in wonder.
compound predicate: The mechanical figures **danced and spun.**

Sometimes the subject of a sentence is difficult to find. In an imperative sentence, the subject is *you*, but it is implied, not written.

(You) Answer the door, please.

You can also place the subject of a sentence after the verb, or between verb parts.

Where is **the manager**?
Where did **she** go?

Practice

Draw one line under the subject of each sentence. Draw two lines under the predicate.

1. Many children need guidance to develop strong moral values.
2. Parents and other relatives must help them decide what's right.
3. Should schools become involved?
4. New Jersey schools focus on and teach character building.
5. A new Oregon program emphasizes honesty, patience, and courage.

COMPLEMENTS

If a predicate includes more than just a verb, it contains a complement. A **complement** is a word that, along with the verb, completes the meaning of the predicate.

The journalist finished **the interview.**

A *direct object* is one kind of complement. Direct objects receive the meaning of action verbs. They answer one of these questions: **whom?** or **what?**

The accountant billed the **client**. (whom?)
The client received an **invoice**. (what?)

An *indirect object* also receives the meaning of an action verb. It answers one of these questions: **to whom? for whom? to what?** or **for what?**

The accountant gave **her assistant** a raise. (to whom?)
My accountant directed me to **this business**. (to what?)

A *subject complement* is a noun or adjective that comes after a linking verb. It renames or describes the subject.

adjective: The lawyer's argument was **clever**.
noun: She is the new **commissioner**.

An *object complement* is a noun or adjective that comes just after a direct object. It renames or describes the direct object.

adjective: Thousands of fans found the performance **unforgettable.**
noun: I considered myself an **amateur.**

Practice

Identify each underlined portion of these sentences as a direct object, an indirect object, a subject complement, or an object complement.

1. A Laundromat is a good <u>place</u> to meet people.
2. Many people have made <u>friends</u> there.
3. People offer <u>strangers help</u> folding clothes.
4. It is a clean, safe <u>environment</u>.
5. Laundromats give <u>people</u> a common <u>chore</u> to share.

CLAUSES

A **clause** is a group of words containing both a subject and a predicate. You use a clause as part of a sentence.

An *independent clause* is one that can stand alone.

The doorbell rang before dinner was over.
When I opened the door, **a salesperson stood there.**

A *dependent clause* includes a subject and predicate but cannot stand alone. It must be joined to an independent clause in a sentence.

I was rather rude **because it was dinnertime.**

An *adjective clause* is a dependent clause that modifies a noun or a pronoun. Most adjective clauses are introduced with a relative pronoun: **who, whom, whose, that,** or **which,** or by a relative adverb: **where, when, why, since,** or **before.**

His goods, **which were unusual,** consisted of strange vitamin concoctions.
They helped people **who felt old or tired.**

An *adverb clause* is a dependent clause that modifies a verb, an adjective, or an adverb. Often, an adverb clause will start with a subordinating conjunction (see page 87).

Since I was rather tired, I bought a few jars.
I took the vitamins **even though I had doubts.**

A *noun clause* is a dependent clause that you use as a noun. Often, you can introduce a noun clause with a pronoun or a subordinating conjunction.

The fact is **that I had a vitamin deficiency.**
The pills replaced **whatever essential vitamins I lacked.**

Practice

Identify each underlined clause as an adjective clause, an adverb clause, a noun clause, or an independent clause.

1. <u>Who will win the election</u> is anyone's guess.
2. The candidates campaigned hard <u>wherever they could</u>.
3. The issues <u>that decided the vote</u> were education and taxes.
4. The conservative candidate, <u>who opposed higher taxes</u>, won the election.
5. <u>The liberal was gracious although he felt bitter</u>.

SENTENCE TYPES

There are four basic types of sentence structure. The first type is a simple sentence. A **simple sentence** includes only a single independent clause.

We always try to please our clients.

A **compound sentence** includes more than one independent clause. The clauses are joined by a comma and a coordinating conjunction, a semicolon, or a semicolon and certain subordinating conjunctions.

> **comma and coordinating conjunction:** You may mail the letter to me, or you may call in the morning.
> **semicolon:** I read your story in one hour; it was the best part of my day.
> **semicolon and subordinating conjunction:** The historical accuracy in your fiction is extraordinary; **however,** you still have to address certain problems in plot development.

A **complex sentence** includes an independent clause and at least one dependent clause.

> Because of the prevalence of bodyguards among celebrities, a movie studio made a film about one.
> The film, which did very well, starred two of Hollywood's most popular actors.

A **compound-complex sentence** includes more than one independent clause and one or more dependent clauses.

> In the film, the bodyguard protects his employer all too well; it was a romantic movie.

Practice

Identify each of these sentences as simple, compound, complex, or compound-complex.

1. Many people think that hot dogs are unhealthy, but they continue to be one of the U.S.A.'s favorite dishes.
2. Most hot dogs, which can be made from beef, pork, or turkey, contain a lot of fat.
3. Hot dogs are also very high in sodium and low in nutritional value.
4. While most people eat hot dogs at ballgames and picnics,

they remain a staple on shopping lists; Americans consume almost 16 billion each year.
5. Luckily, some brands are now low-fat and low in sodium, and they even taste good.

In this chapter, you learned about the four different kinds of sentences: declarative, interrogative, imperative, and exclamatory. You discovered that sentences are made up of subjects and predicates, learned where and what an object is, and found out how to use clauses. Finally, you explored the four types of sentence structures: simple, compound, complex, and compound-complex. This knowledge will help you to create interesting, informative sentences when you get down to the actual work of writing.

7

Developing Paragraphs

- *TOPIC SENTENCES*
- *SUPPORTING DETAILS*
- *PARAGRAPH UNITY AND COHERENCE*
- *INTRODUCTORY PARAGRAPHS*
- *CONCLUDING PARAGRAPHS*

The paragraph mark, ¶, is a Greek symbol. Ancient Greeks placed it in the margin next to the place in their writing where they felt the reader should pause. Now we indent paragraphs, but the intent is the same. A paragraph is a group of sentences that expresses a thought or idea. At the end of a paragraph, the reader pauses before going on to the next paragraph.

TOPIC SENTENCES

A **topic sentence** is a sentence that expresses the *main idea* of a paragraph. It tells what the paragraph is about. A topic sentence can appear anywhere in a paragraph; most often, it occurs at the start or the end. If you put your topic sentence at the beginning of the paragraph, it tells your readers what to expect as they read. If you place it at the end, it sums up your main idea.

With the problems in the ozone layer, consumers and manufacturers are more concerned than ever with developing sunscreens that work. One in six Americans will get skin cancer, so skin care companies are coming out with higher SPF products. They are also developing products that protect against both UVA and UVB radiation.

Since the development of effective sunscreens, Americans have been spending more time than ever in the sun. Unfortunately, until recently, most sunscreens protected only against UVB radiation. Some scientists contend that the growing incidence of melanoma is the result of increased exposure to UVA rays that these products do not screen.

Practice

Find the topic sentence in each of these paragraphs. In your own words, tell the main idea of the paragraph.

1. In New York City, a boy named Keron fell in love with the subway. He rode it constantly and was so fond of riding that he befriended a motorman and convinced him that he too was a driver. Keron's whole aim in life was to drive a subway train.
2. Keron achieved his dangerous dream. He signed on as his friend for a shift and took control of the train. He drove it to Brooklyn safely, but on the way back he went too fast and set off the emergency brake. Keron fled the scene; police tracked him down days later.

SUPPORTING DETAILS

In a paragraph, all of the sentences should support the main idea. The type of supporting details you use will differ depending on the type of writing you are doing. You can use **descrip-**

tive details, or details that appeal to the five senses. Descriptive details are most useful in narrative writing or writing that describes.

> The room had a sterile, antiseptic feel to it. The walls were bright white, the lighting was fluorescent, and the floor tiles were so clean they could be used as mirrors. The few pieces of furniture were metal. It smelled of cleaning fluid, and I got the feeling that if I spoke, my voice would echo back to me.

Another kind of detail is the **example.** Examples provide specific incidents or evidence to support a main idea. They're most useful in informative or persuasive writing.

> Daily life can be frustrating for toddlers. They often can't speak clearly enough to make their wants and needs known. Their physical abilities, especially their fine motor skills, can get in the way of activities they long to perform. One toddler, desperate to fit an octagonal block into a hole, shrieked for half an hour when his fingers just couldn't control their movements enough for success.

You can also support your main idea by using **facts** or **statistics.** Words and numbers that back up your topic strengthen many kinds of nonfiction and business writing. Facts and statistics are most useful in persuasive or explanatory writing.

> The biggest animal that ever lived has recently been unearthed in Utah. It's a dinosaur called Seismosaurus, and it was nearly 140 feet in length. That's 40 feet longer than the largest blue whale. A Seismosaurus was so big that it may have had multiple hearts to move the blood through its enormous body.

Practice

Write a paragraph on each of these main ideas. Use the type of supporting details suggested.

1. The best music for dancing is [your favorite]. Develop with examples.
2. A piece of machinery can be beautiful. Develop with descriptive details.
3. Low-fat diets are healthy. Develop with facts and statistics.

PARAGRAPH UNITY AND COHERENCE

In a paragraph, you achieve **unity** when all of your detail sentences support the main idea. This paragraph is not unified. Can you tell why?

> The prospect of retirement strikes terror into the hearts of some nearly senior citizens. What will they do with all their spare time? Will their savings allow them to live comfortably? Retirement can be a time of great freedom. Not everyone enjoys it, though.

As you can see, the last two sentences do not support the main idea, which is that some people are scared of retiring. The writer would do well to delete these sentences and include further examples of worries that people have about retirement.

You achieve paragraph **coherence** when your detail sentences are arranged in a logical order that the reader can easily follow. There are several different methods of arranging sentences. One way is in **chronological order.** When you use chronological order, you place events in the order in which they occur. This method of organization is especially useful in explaining or in some narratives.

> To get yourself a job interview, you should first find out if your target company is hiring. Call up and determine to whom you should send your résumé. Then send it, along with a well-written cover letter. Finally, a follow-up phone call will ensure that the résumé has been received and read.

Spatial order is another way to organize details. This type of organization works well in descriptions or directions. You can organize spatially from left to right, right to left, top to bottom, bottom to top, near to far, or far to near.

> He stared at the creature in amazement. It had enormous feet clad in huge black shoes, and legs that seemed to extend for yards. Its chest was twice the size of his, and its shoulders twice as broad. A jaw that beat out Schwarzenegger's, red hair that sprang out in all directions—*this* was his new son-in-law?

You can arrange details by *comparing and contrasting*. When you do this, you cite similarities and differences between two things. This method of organization works well in explanations. You can arrange comparison and contrast writing in two ways.

1. You can present all the details on one subject first, then all the details on the other subject.

> Gas grills are usually easy to light, and they cook evenly. It doesn't matter if the weather is bad when you're cooking with gas. A charcoal grill, on the other hand, gives food that true grilled taste, but charcoal can be cranky in damp weather, and if the coals aren't arranged well, they can cook unevenly.

2. You can compare and contrast your subjects detail by detail.

> King Charles and Prince Charles spaniels do possess some important differences. King Charles spaniels are black and tan, while the Prince Charles is tricolored—white, black, and tan. The Prince Charles has spots over its eyes and on its muzzle, chest, and legs, but the King Charles is not spotted.

If you are writing persuasively—an editorial, for example— you may wish to arrange your details in *order of importance*. When you use this method, you put the most important detail or reason first.

Students should be given control of the university newspaper. They must be allowed to practice freedom of speech and to come up against the problems and pitfalls of this First Amendment right. They should have the opportunity to exercise the sort of job responsibility they will face in daily life after graduation. They don't need to answer to faculty—after all, they're adults, aren't they?

Organization by *cause and effect* will help you in writing some research papers or other nonfiction. You can begin with a cause and explain how it leads to an effect or effects, or you can begin with an effect and explain its cause or causes.

cause   As stars shrink, their atoms crowd closer together, and move faster and faster. The interior, or core, begins to heat up. At a certain crucial temperature, a large star will explode, becoming a

effect   supernova.

You can clarify movement from sentence to sentence within a paragraph, or from paragraph to paragraph, by using *transitions*. A transition shows how one sentence or idea is linked to another. Without transitions, your writing will seem choppy or confusing (or both). Using transitions well lets your ideas flow easily and clearly. Here are some common transitional words.

chronological order: first, next, then, last, finally, meanwhile
spatial order: above, below, behind, in front, beneath
summing up: therefore, thus, in other words, consequently
qualifying: usually, specifically, frequently, even if
explaining: because, for, since
restricting: however, although, if, unless, when

Practice

Write a paragraph for each topic given. Organize the paragraph as suggested. Include transitions in your paragraph.

1. Describe something that happened to you last weekend. Use chronological order.
2. Describe a room in your home. Use spatial order.
3. Explain why you prefer foreign cars to American cars, or vice versa. Use comparison and contrast.
4. Explain why recycling should be mandatory. Use order of importance.
5. Explain what happens to you when you watch MTV. Use cause and effect order.

INTRODUCTORY PARAGRAPHS

One of the purposes of an **introductory paragraph,** no matter what sort of writing you are doing, is to grab the interest of your readers. There are several ways you can do this.

1. You can **ask a question.**

Is there such as thing as the "wolf child"? There are many incidences of children reported to have been raised by animals, but scientists doubt that a child could survive without any human contact.

2. You can begin **with a quote.**

"Man's inhumanity to man," wrote the poet Robert Burns, "makes countless thousands mourn." This is nowhere more true than in what used to be Yugoslavia.

3. You can begin **with an unusual fact.**

An average-size adult human being has at least six pounds of bacteria inside his or her body. You'd think we would all be deathly ill—but many of these bacteria are useful rather than harmful.

4. You can begin **with a striking description**.

> The sky was boiling as if it had been heated on a giant stove. Gray clouds bubbled as the wind whipped them in circles and sent them scudding toward the horizon.

Practice

Write an introductory paragraph on each of these topics. Use one of the techniques suggested.

1. Describe your favorite city. Begin with a quotation or a striking description.
2. Discuss salaries of sports stars. Begin with a question or an unusual fact.

CONCLUDING PARAGRAPHS

Just as it is important to write an interesting first paragraph, it is vital to write a **concluding paragraph** that ties your piece together. Here are some techniques to help you end your writing.

1. You can **restate your argument.** This method works well for persuasive writing. It clarifies what you have argued and sums up your reasons.

> It is clear that we need more primary care doctors. The percentage of general practitioners and internists has shrunk by 25 percent in the past 30 years. This has led to increased costs and a lack of basic care for many. If health care reform is to succeed, it must address this pressing problem.

2. You can **end chronologically.** If you are writing a narrative, this type of ending often works well.

The wind finally stopped. From their burrow in the snowbank, Hank and Lenny heard the world return to normalcy. They dug their way up to air, through almost a foot of new snow. When they broke through the crust, Hank started to laugh, but Lenny just stared. There, not ten yards away, was their own house.

3. You can **summarize what you have said.** This type of conclusion is best for much nonfiction and business writing.

In short, updating our office phone system would help to increase both orders and efficiency. A single receptionist would route calls, an 800 number would increase orders, and a special number for customer assistance would lead to customer satisfaction and, as a result, higher volume.

Practice

Write a concluding paragraph for each of these topics. Use the technique suggested.

1. a dreadful vacation (end chronologically)
2. the placement of homeless shelters (summarize)
3. abuse of privacy by news reporters (restate argument)

You've learned how to construct a paragraph—the foundation and walls of your house of words. You can develop a main idea, write a topic sentence, and use supporting details. You can write an introduction, use transitions, and compose a conclusion. These skills are the basis for most types of writing.

8

Aspects of Style

- *PURPOSE AND AUDIENCE*
- *TONE*
- *LANGUAGE LEVELS*
- *POINT OF VIEW*
- *ALLUSIONS*
- *FIGURATIVE LANGUAGE*

Once you have addressed the basics of words, sentences, and paragraphs, you can begin developing style in your writing. Your style may differ according to whom you are writing for and what type of writing you are doing.

PURPOSE AND AUDIENCE

One thing you can be sure of every time you write is that you will have a **purpose.** Your purpose is your reason for writing. If you dash off a postcard to a friend, your purpose might be to tell her what a wonderful vacation you are having. If you write a report on the growing of grapes in winemaking, your purpose might be to explain the way grapes are grown. Common purposes include the following:

to entertain: This will be your purpose most frequently in fiction writing.

to explain or inform: When you write nonfiction or for business reasons, you will often be writing to explain or inform.

to persuade: Newspaper and magazine editorials, some reviews, and some letters and reports have persuasion as their purpose.

to express your opinion, thoughts, or feelings: You will do most of your personal writing for this purpose.

to analyze: Analytical writing focuses on the subject and addresses the question *why?* or *how?* You will often combine an analytical purpose with explaining or persuading. However, when you analyze, you do not focus on your reader's understanding; you concentrate on your subject.

You should also keep in mind your **audience,** or for whom you are writing. Your audience may be yourself, a business associate, a teacher, your class, your community, or an unknown group of readers. Sometimes, though not always, your audience will make a difference in your style. For example, if you are writing a magazine article on ulcers, your style will be different if your audience is readers of *Time* magazine than if it is readers of the *New England Journal of Medicine*. When you consider your audience, ask yourself these questions.

1. How much does my audience know about my topic?
2. What aspects of my topic will interest my audience most?
3. What information will my audience need to understand my topic?

Your answers will help you determine what information to include in your writing.

TONE

The **tone** of your writing is the attitude you express toward your subject and your audience. Certain types of writing should display only an objective, informative tone. These include most of your business writing and certain types of nonfiction writing. Other tones you might use include *ironic, angry, sarcastic, sentimental, ribald,* or *flattering.* There are as many tones as there are types of and reasons for writing.

Your purpose and your audience should help to determine your tone. For example, if you are writing up the minutes to a meeting, you may want to use an objective tone. If you are composing a letter to the editor about the odors from a nearby sewage treatment plant, your tone may be angry, concerned, or sarcastic.

LANGUAGE LEVELS

When you consider your purpose, audience, and tone, you will have an idea of the **level of language** and the types of words you will want to use. You can write in *formal English,* in which your grammar is scrupulously correct, your sentences are longer, and your tone is serious. You can write in *informal English,* in which your sentences are shorter and your tone is more casual. Informal English may contain **idioms,** or words and phrases that have evolved into a meaning different from their dictionary definition or strictly grammatical usage.

My cousin was **carrying on** about the accident.
He **had his hands full** with the twins.
Who's there? **It's just me.**

Informal English may also include *slang,* words or phrases that are given new, usually temporary meanings.

We had a **wild** night.
That dress looks **fresh** on you.

Here are suggested language levels for various types of writing.

formal	**informal**
business writing	friendly letter
research paper	journal entry
some journalism	some journalism
formal speeches	some fiction writing

Under most circumstances, you will want to avoid using *jargon,* or specialized words and phrases, in your writing. If you are writing an article on the manufacture of CDs for an audience of CD manufacturers, you can use jargon because your readers will understand it. If the article is for readers of your local newspaper, however, you will want to keep the specialized language to a minimum. Jargon should only be used when you are certain your audience will understand it, and even then you should use as little as possible.

POINT OF VIEW

The **point of view** of a story is the vantage point from which it is told. There are several points of view you can use in fiction writing.

first-person point of view: The narrator is a part of the story and is referred to as "I."

limited third-person point of view: The narrator's view of the action is limited, usually to one character. The reader only knows what that character sees, thinks, and feels.

omniscient third-person point of view: The narrator sees everything that happens.

When you are writing fiction, your choice of point of view is very important. A reader's understanding and impression of your characters and plot will vary greatly depending on your narrator and what he or she can see.

Practice

Read the passage. Identify the point of view. Then rewrite it using a different point of view.

"Did you mean what you said yesterday?" Jamie asked, almost casually. "Is there a job open here?"
    I looked at him carefully. His glance was unconcerned, but his hands twisted together. He was clearly nervous.
    "Think you can keep up?" I inquired, equally casual.

ALLUSIONS

An **allusion** is a reference to a person, place, or thing that possesses associated meanings. You can use allusions to clarify images or to explain without going into detail.

They looked **like hippies**, but this was the nineties, not the sixties.

The term "hippie" conjures up an image in the reader's mind, and the writer does not have to provide further description.

The movie wants to portray a modern-day **Lost Generation.**

This sentence alludes to the "Lost Generation," the generation of restless, purposeless artists and writers who came of age after World War I.

FIGURATIVE LANGUAGE

Figurative language is language that imaginatively invokes a comparison. You use figurative language to describe things by using comparisons. It enriches your writing by helping you create images in your readers' minds.

A **simile** is a comparison that uses the words **like** or **as.**

They ran **like** the wind.
He seemed tall **as** a mountain.

A **metaphor** compares without using **like** or **as.**

The road was a silvery ribbon, winding itself between the hills.

Personification is a comparison that gives a nonhuman subject human traits.

The desert slumbered in the hot noon sun.

In this sentence, the writer gives the desert the human quality of sleeping. It is not really sleeping, of course, but the comparison conjures an image of a very quiet, restful place.

Practice

Write a description of one of these subjects. Use at least two kinds of figurative language.

1. A tornado
2. A Victorian mansion
3. A threatening supervisor
4. An old automobile

You have learned various ways in which to develop your writing style. The way you use tone, allusions, and figurative language, and the language level, audience, and purpose you choose, all contribute to the overall style of each piece of writing you do.

9

Special Problems in Grammar and Usage

- *SUBJECT-VERB AGREEMENT*
- *MODIFIER PROBLEMS*
- *PRONOUN PROBLEMS*
- *VERB PROBLEMS*
- *PREPOSITIONAL AND INFINITIVE PROBLEMS*
- *SENTENCE PROBLEMS*
- *SEXIST LANGUAGE*
- *TROUBLESOME WORDS*

Even after you've learned the rules for correct grammar and usage, you might still run into writing trouble every now and then. This chapter will address the most common problems writers face in using language correctly.

SUBJECT-VERB AGREEMENT

Your subject and your verb must agree in number. When the subject of a sentence is singular, the verb must be singular, and when the subject is plural, the verb must be plural. A singular verb ends in -*s*. A plural verb usually does not end in -*s*.

singular: The parachutist **opens** her chute.
plural: The planes **drop** dozens of skydivers.

Subject-verb agreement often becomes a problem when the subject and verb are separated by other words.

wrong: Each of the teachers **carry** a placard.
right: Each of the teachers **carries** a placard.

The subject in this sentence is **each.** The words *of the teachers* are a prepositional phrase. If you look at the sentence without the prepositional phrase, the subject-verb agreement becomes clearer: Each **carries** a placard.

Phrases beginning with words such as *except, in addition to, including,* and *together with* can also confuse subject-verb agreement.

wrong: The gymnast, together with his coach, **are** going to Austin.
right: The gymnast, together with his coach, **is** going to Austin.

The subject is the gymnast, which is singular, so you should use the singular verb **is.**

Subject-verb agreement can be complicated by conjunctions. If the conjunction *and* creates a compound subject, you should use a plural verb.

The catcher and the runner **were** injured in the play.

When you join subjects with the conjunctions *or, nor, either → or,* or *neither → nor,* the verb should agree with the subject nearest to it.

Either Janet or **Yuri cooks** every night.
Neither Thomas nor **Harry and I eat** much at dinner.

Collective nouns can be confusing when you try to make them agree with a verb. If the group described in the noun acts as a single unit, you will use it as a singular noun. If the group acts individually, you will use the noun as a plural.

singular: The family **vacations** at the same place each year.
plural:　 The family **organize** their campsite very quickly.

When a subject refers to an amount that is a single unit, the verb should be singular. If the amount is counted individually, the verb should be plural.

Ten dollars **is** a great price for those shoes.
Ten dollars **are** all the change I could get.

When your subject is an indefinite pronoun, you must give special thought to the number of your verb. Some indefinite pronouns are singular.

another	anybody
anyone	anything
each	either
everybody	everyone
everything	much
neither	nobody
no one	nothing
one	somebody
someone	something

Anyone **knows** the answer to that problem.

Some indefinite pronouns are plural: *both, few, many, several*.

Few of the class **graduate** with honors.

Some indefinite pronouns can be either singular or plural: *all, any, more, most, none,* and *some*.

singular: Some of the test **is** easy.
plural: Some of the students **leave** early.

In some sentences, the subject occurs after the verb. To make sure the subject and verb agree, turn the sentence around in your head, putting the subject first.

There are the owners of the house. (The **owners** of the house **are** there.)
Do the Winthrops plan to move? (The **Winthrops do** plan to move.)

Practice

Rewrite the sentences in which the subject and verb do not agree.

1. The office are holding the yearly picnic.
2. Everyone, from management to mail clerk, go to the event.
3. The secretaries and the executives compete in volleyball.
4. Either the boss or his associates tends the grill.
5. Here are the area where the foot race and long jump take place.

MODIFIER PROBLEMS

One of the main problems you may have when using modifiers is the **double negative.** This occurs when you use two negatives and only one is needed. Remember that contractions can be negative if they include a contracted form of *not* (*n't*). Here are some common negatives.

barely	hardly	never	no	nobody	
none	no one	not	nothing	nowhere	scarcely

wrong: Loni **hasn't hardly** touched her lunch.
right: Loni has **hardly** touched her lunch.
wrong: We **didn't** order **no** takeout food.
right: We **didn't** order **any** takeout food.

The modifiers *good* and *well* can be confusing. You should always use *good* as an adjective.

wrong: He played **good** on the recording.
right: He was a **good** saxophonist.

You can use *well* as either an adjective or an adverb.

adjective: Norah felt **well** again after the course of antibiotics.
adverb: Tammy performed **well** in the play.

Practice

Read these sentences. Rewrite the ones in which modifiers are used incorrectly.

1. The repairperson couldn't fix the washing machine.
2. It still hardly gets none of the clothes clean.
3. The machine worked good at first.
4. After a few months, though, the spin cycle didn't revolve no more.
5. I won't never buy that brand again.

A **misplaced modifier** is a modifier that is placed too far from the word it modifies, resulting in confusion. To correct this, move the modifier closer to the word it modifies.

wrong: Carl ate his ice cream while the TV newscasters recited the day's events **in bed.**
right: Carl ate his ice cream **in bed** while the TV newscasters recited the day's events.

A **dangling modifier** is one whose referent is not clear or is missing from the sentence. Correct this problem by adding or clarifying the reference for the modifier.

wrong: **Before jumping on the bungee cord,** the onlookers applauded her.

right: **Before she jumped on the bungee cord,** the onlookers applauded her.

A **squinting modifier** is one that could modify either of two sentence parts. To correct this, move the modifier so it clearly modifies only one part of the sentence.

wrong: The chef being congratulated warmly thanked the patrons.

right: The chef being congratulated thanked the patrons warmly.

right: The chef being warmly congratulated thanked the patrons.

Practice

Correct each of these awkward modifier placements by moving or changing the modifier.

1. The neighborhood in spring wakes up early on weekends.
2. Full of civic pride, the lawnmowers are pushed by homeowners.
3. Most people have elaborate flower beds with large yards.
4. The bags of peat moss and gardening instruments show that the gardeners work hard.
5. The house next door boasts a vegetable garden, where a retired admiral lives.

PRONOUN PROBLEMS

The main problem writers have with pronouns is antecedent confusion. When you use a pronoun, be sure it refers to a single antecedent. You can clarify a pronoun's antecedent by placing the two close together.

wrong: Jack told Philip that **he** needed to get more exercise.

right: To Philip, Jack said that **he** needed to get more exercise.

wrong: Theresa and Joan went shopping. **She** needed a new suit.

right: Theresa and Joan went shopping. **They** needed new suits.

When you use demonstrative pronouns, be sure their antecedents are clear.

wrong: I have brown eyes, curly hair, and freckles. **That** is determined genetically.

right: I have brown eyes, curly hair, and freckles. **Those** are genetically determined traits.

When you use a pronoun, be sure it agrees in number with its antecedent.

wrong: A senior citizen often worries about **their** pension.

right: Senior citizens often worry about **their** pensions.

When antecedents are made plural with the conjunction *and*, use a plural pronoun.

My brother **and** sister drive **their** cars everywhere.

If the antecedents are linked by *or* or *nor*, the pronoun should agree with the closest antecedent.

Neither my brother **nor** my sister will lend **her** car.

If you use a singular indefinite pronoun, be sure any referring pronoun is singular.

Everyone at the party tested **his** or **her** skill.

If you use a plural indefinite pronoun, be sure any referring pronoun is plural.

Most won **themselves** a prize.

If you use a collective noun, a referring pronoun should match the noun's number.

The group is having **its** weekly luncheon.
The group are preparing **their** fundraising activities.

Be sure you use the correct form of a pronoun. If a pronoun is used in place of a subject or follows the verb *to be*, it is in the *nominative case*.

nominative pronouns: I, he, she, you, they, who

If a pronoun is used as a direct or indirect object, it is in the *objective case*.

objective pronouns: me, him, her, you, them, whom

wrong: It was a private conversation between Jack and **I**.
right: It was a private conversation between Jack and **me**.
wrong: To **who** should I address the envelope?
right: To **whom** should I address the envelope?

Practice

Rewrite these sentences so the pronouns match their antecedents and are used correctly.

1. It was them who volunteers to raise money.
2. The homeless are people whom need our help.

3. Neither the federal government nor the local government will give us their help.
4. People at the meeting offered his or her time and money.
5. Everybody there was a credit to their community.

VERB PROBLEMS

One of the biggest problems writers face in verb use is overuse of the passive voice (for more information on the passive voice, see page 67). When you use the passive voice, the subject of your sentence receives the verb's action. This tends to weaken your writing, by making actions less direct. In general, try to keep your verbs active by making your subject perform the verb's action. Using the passive voice also allows a writer to omit the actor who is performing the action; politicians are notorious for doing this, as a way to minimize or avoid responsibility.

passive: Mistakes **were made** by the Oval Office.
active: The Oval Office **made** mistakes.

Another common problem is shifts in verb tense. Usually, you should be consistent in the tense you use. If your action takes place in the present, keep it in the present. If it takes place in the past, keep it in the past.

The violinist **is** warming up as the orchestra **begins** to tune their instruments.

However, sometimes a logical shift in verb tense is necessary. If events occur at different times, you may have to refer to them in different tenses.

The violinist **had prepared** for weeks. Now she **waits** in the wings, tense with anticipation.

Practice

Correct each of these sentences. Make passive verbs active, and change verb tenses so they make logical sense.

1. Settlers travel along the Oregon Trail, which is now a tourist attraction.
2. American Indians were victimized by many of the settlers.
3. In Oregon, Narcissa and Marcus Whitman were killed by Native Americans.
4. The Indians died by the thousand of measles, but the Whitmans remain healthy.
5. In desperation and fear, the Indians attack the settlers, who were not defended by the militia.

PREPOSITIONAL AND INFINITIVE PROBLEMS

Without noticing, you might use extra prepositions when you speak. This is a common error in speech, and few people notice it. But be sure that you don't make the same mistake in your writing.

wrong:	The skier hopped off **of** the lift.
right:	The skier hopped off the lift.
wrong:	Where is that bus going **to?**
right:	Where is that bus going?

Practice

Rewrite these sentences so the prepositions are correct.

1. Where is the ship sailing to?
2. The passengers ask the purser where their cabins are at.
3. At once they begin to drink champagne as the ship moves off of its mooring.

SENTENCE PROBLEMS

There are three requirements for a complete sentence: it must have a subject, it must have a predicate verb, and it must contain a complete thought. If any one of these requirements is not met, you have written a *sentence fragment.* You can correct a sentence fragment simply by supplying the missing sentence part.

missing subject:	Just couldn't find the concert hall.
correction:	I just couldn't find the concert hall.
missing verb:	The opera star singing with the chorus.
correction:	The opera star was singing with the chorus.
incomplete thought:	Even though there were other performers.
correction:	Even though there were other performers, the star stood out.

Another common problem you might encounter in sentence writing is the *run-on.* A run-on consists of two or more sentences that are written as one. You can correct this by dividing the sentences using conjunctions, semicolons, or periods. (For more information on using semicolons and periods, see pages 127–128 and page 135.)

wrong:	The tryouts were on Saturday Tina could hardly wait.
right:	The tryouts were on Saturday. Tina could hardly wait.
wrong:	She prepared the part carefully, she was sure she would get it.
right:	She prepared the part carefully; she was sure she would get it.

Practice

Rewrite this paragraph, correcting any sentence fragments or run-on sentences.

The Brooklyn Bridge is a masterpiece of engineering, it connects Brooklyn to Manhattan. The product of intense labor. Many lives lost during its building. Now, though it shows its age a bit, it is a beautiful sight to see as evening turns to night. All lit up. Walking from one end to the other at dusk is a great experience, everyone who visits New York should try it.

SEXIST LANGUAGE

During the last few decades, people have become increasingly aware of sexism in our society. We are more careful about not promoting sexism in schools, in the workplace, and in society as a whole. As a reflection of this awareness, it is important to watch for and eliminate sexist language in your writing. A common problem for writers trying to avoid sexist language is the question of pronoun usage. For a long time, writers used the pronouns **he, him,** and **his** to refer to people of unidentified gender. The easiest way to solve this problem is to substitute the plural pronoun—**they, them,** and **their**—when possible. When it is not, use the more awkward **he or she [she or he], him or her,** and **his or hers.**

wrong: Any car owner knows that **he** has to maintain **his** vehicle.

right: Any car owner knows that **he or she** has to maintain **his or her** vehicle.

right: Car owners know that **they** have to maintain **their** vehicles.

The same rule holds true when you are using pronouns that imply gender assumptions: **Don't.** Don't assume that all secretaries are women; don't assume that all plumbers are men.

wrong: A good nurse gets to know **her** patients personally.

right: Good nurses get to know **their** patients personally.

wrong: A construction worker must never forget **his** hardhat.

right: A construction worker must never forget **his or her** hardhat.

You should avoid use of the universal masculine term, *man*, and its offshoots, such as *mankind, congressman*, and *chairman*. You should also watch for terms that are limited to women. Here are some common gender-specific terms and their nonsexist replacements.

man	→	person, human
mankind	→	humankind
fireman	→	fire fighter
businessman	→	businessperson
mailman	→	mail carrier
actress	→	actor
policeman	→	police officer
housewife	→	homemaker
stewardess	→	flight attendant
chairman	→	chair
coed	→	student
waitress	→	waiter

Practice

Rewrite these sentences so they do not contain sexist language.

1. The chairman of the history department made a speech last week.
2. He felt that none of the athletes in history classes was doing as well as he should.
3. He wanted each of the coaches to provide extra tutoring for his athletes.

4. Several of the coeds objected to his ideas.
5. They felt that whether a person was an athlete or a housewife, her background shouldn't be blamed for her grades.

TROUBLESOME WORDS

Words that sound alike or have similar spellings but are different in meaning can pose a problem for writers. It is important to use these words correctly so readers can understand what you are saying. Here are some common troublesome words.

all ready, already: **All ready** means *prepared*.
Already means *before or by this time*.
Mr. Chang was **all ready** to begin the meeting.
He had **already** briefed everyone on the topic under discussion.

among, between: **Among** refers to *more than two things*.
Between refers to *two things*.
Lawrence sat **between** his brother and sister.
Their red hair stood out **among** the dark heads around them.

bring, take: **Bring** means *to come with* or *to carry to*.
Take means *to go with* or *to carry away*.
Johanna will **bring** dessert to the party.
She can **take** home the leftovers.

can, may: **Can** indicates *ability*.
May indicates *permission*.
Tory **can** swim over a mile without stopping.
May she come to the pool with me today?

effect, affect: Effect means *the result.*
Affect means *to influence.*
The play had a strong **effect** on José.
It **affected** him so much he couldn't speak.

except, accept: Except means *other than.*
Accept means *to agree to* or *to approve of.*
Everyone went to the dance **except** Tiffany.
She would not **accept** any invitations.

farther, further: Farther means *more distant.*
Further means *more.*
I believe the campground is just a little **farther**.
I'd better give the map **further** study.

fewer, less: Use **fewer** with nouns that you count.
Use **less** with nouns you cannot count.
There are **fewer** people at the rally than expected.
It will make **less** of an impact than we'd hoped.

lay, lie: Lay means *to put;* use it with a direct object.
Lie means *to be put.*
Lay the dress on the ironing board.
Don't let it **lie** there for days.

lain, laid: Lain is the past participle of *lie.*
Laid is the past tense of *lay.*
The dog had **lain** by the fire all day.
Before he went out, he **laid** his bone down carefully.

learn, teach: Learn means *to receive instruction.*
Teach means *to give instruction.*
Gina wanted to **learn** Russian.
She asked Rebekah to **teach** her.

real, really: Real means *true* or *genuine*.
Really means *actually*.
The birthday party was a **real** surprise.
Stephanie was **really** shocked.

rise, raise: Rise means *to move upward*.
Raise means *to be moved upward;* use it with a direct object.
As the overture ended, the curtain began to **rise**.
The stage manager **raised** it.

sit, set: Sit means *to occupy a seat*.
Set takes a direct object and means *to put*.
Won't you **sit** down, Mr. Turku?
Just **set** your briefcase on that table.

than, then: Use **than** in comparisons.
Then means *next*.
For sixteen years, Jen was taller **than** her twin John.
Then John grew five inches.

way, ways: Use **way** to refer to distance.
Use **ways** only as the plural of *way*.
This road goes on for a long **way**.
There are several **ways** we could get there.

hopefully: Hopefully is often misused to mean *with hope*
or *I hope*. It means *full of hope*.
wrong: **Hopefully,** we'll win the lottery.
right: **Hopefully,** we listened to the lottery drawing.

a lot: A lot is always written as two words.
Simka likes her job **a lot**.

like: Like is often misused to mean *as*. It is also incorrectly used as emphasis.

wrong: **Like** my mother used to say, "You can pick your friends, but you can't pick your family."

wrong: My brother-in-law is, **like,** a real loser.

right: Keith got rollerblades just **like** his friend's.

different from: Different from is often written as *different than*. This is incorrect.

The movie was **different from** the book.

should, would, could have: These are often incorrectly written as *should of, would of*, and *could of*.

Joan **should have** taken the bus home.

She **would have** if she **could have** left work earlier.

Practice

Choose the correct word in parentheses to complete each sentence.

1. The Cruzes were (all ready, already) to leave on vacation.
2. The whole family was going (accept, except) for the dog.
3. They were carrying (alot, a lot) of luggage.
4. The airport was (further, farther) than they'd thought.
5. They had to walk a long (ways, way) to the terminal.
6. The baby was so tired he wanted to (lay, lie) on the conveyer belt.
7. Everyone felt (real, really) exhausted.
8. The airline had booked more passengers than they should (have, of).
9. Luckily, (less, fewer) of them turned up (then, than) expected.
10. The Cruzes were seated (among, between) the two aisles.

You're now aware of some of the biggest pitfalls writers face. You can use parts of speech correctly, and you know when a sentence is not a sentence—and when it's too much of one. You can recognize sexist language and you know how to use troublesome words. This knowledge puts you one up on most people. You can use it to refine and correct your writing—*and* you can take great pleasure in catching public figures making the errors you've learned to avoid.

III

Punctuation, Capitalization, and Spelling

10

Rules of Punctuation

- *ENDING SENTENCES*
- *USING COMMAS*
- *PUNCTUATING TITLES*
- *USING QUOTATION MARKS*
- *USING SEMICOLONS, COLONS, AND DASHES*
- *USING APOSTROPHES*
- *USING PARENTHESES AND ELLIPSES*

You've learned how to use the rules of grammar to build sentences. Now you need to know how to punctuate the sentences you write. The meaning of your words can change, depending on what punctuation you use. If used incorrectly, punctuation can make your writing incomprehensible. If used correctly, it can enhance and complete your writing.

ENDING SENTENCES

There are three punctuation marks you can use to end a sentence. The first and most common of these is the *period*. Use a period to end a declarative sentence.

Jane rode the elevator to the eighty-second floor.

Use a period to end most imperative sentences.

Get off the elevator, please.

Use a *question mark* to end a question, or interrogative sentence.

What is wrong with this elevator?

If you write an interrogative sentence within another sentence, include the question mark at the end of the interrogative sentence.

Did the help button work? was the question on Jane's mind.

Use an *exclamation point* to end an exclamatory sentence and some imperative sentences.

Help! This elevator is stuck!
Push the help button now!

Be careful about overusing exclamation points. Only use them when necessary to indicate emphasis. Never use more than one following a sentence.

Practice

Choose the appropriate end punctuation for each of these sentences.

1. The child was terrified of the water
2. Had he fallen in when he was a baby
3. Watch out for the slippery rocks
4. No one is sure just what happened
5. Save the baby

USING COMMAS

A **comma** indicates a pause in your sentence. There are many rules for using commas, but a good rule of thumb is that if you would pause when speaking, you probably need a comma. It often helps to read something aloud if you're not sure whether to use a comma.

Use a comma for joining the two clauses in a compound sentence.

> The commencement ceremonies were long, and the sun was very hot.

Use a comma to separate three or more words or phrases in a series.

> The students, their parents, and the officials grew warmer and warmer.

Use a comma to separate two or more adjectives, unless the second adjective is used in combination with a noun.

> The wilting, exhausted seniors wanted the ceremony to end.
> Their long black robes were stifling.

Use a comma to set off a noun of direct address.

> Seniors, welcome to your lives!

Use a comma when you add an abbreviated title after a person's name. If the name is within a sentence, use a comma after the abbreviation.

> Richard Myers, Ph.D., spoke about life after graduation.

Use a comma to set off quotations from explanatory words that tell who speaks in what manner.

> Myers asked, "Does anyone here plan to fail?"
> "Not us," the audience replied in unison, "not us!"

Use a comma to set off a nonrestrictive dependent adverb clause that follows the main clause.

The speeches were long, although the speakers were uncomfortable.

Use a comma to set off a dependent adverb clause that comes before the main clause.

When the last speech was made, the applause was weak.

Use a comma after an adverb phrase unless it is very short or falls just before the verb.

Because of the heat, several people fainted.
For decades it had rained at graduation.
On the platform stood the graduating class.

Use a comma to set off a nonrestrictive adjective phrase that follows the noun and does not change its meaning.

The sky, which had been blue, suddenly filled with gray thunderclouds.

Use a comma after a participial phrase that begins a sentence, unless it falls just before the verb.

Looking nervously at the sky, the audience shuffled in their seats.
Ascending the steps was the university president.

Use a comma after two or more prepositional phrases that begin a sentence.

Because the wind blew before the storm, he shivered suddenly.

Use a comma to set off exclamations and certain adverbs, if they indicate a pause.

He hadn't noticed, however, that the weather had changed.
My, did he jump when the thunderclap came!

Set off an appositive with commas unless it is restrictive.

The shock caused the master of ceremonies, Dr. Hatcher, to collapse.
Her husband Harry rushed to her aid.

Use a comma to avoid confusion in your sentences.

wrong: Above the sky grew more threatening.
right: Above, the sky grew more threatening.

Use a comma to separate measurements written as words.

The stage was eight feet, six inches above the ground.

Use commas to separate the elements in an address. When the address is within a sentence, place a comma after the state or country.

The college is located at 204 Wilson Street, Albuquerque, New Mexico.
Albuquerque, New Mexico, is a fast-expanding city.

Use commas to separate the numbers in a date. When the date is within a sentence, put a comma after the year.

Commencement took place on May 23, 199-.
May 23, 199-, was an important day in my life.

Use a comma after the greeting of a personal letter and after the closing of any letter.

Dear Grandmother,
Sincerely yours,

Practice

Rewrite the following sentences, placing commas where they are needed.

1. The farmer's market a local institution is a great place to shop.
2. There are stands selling vegetables preserves and pastries.
3. From miles away in all sorts of conveyances people come to sell their goods.
4. Many of the vendors it seems never left the sixties.
5. They dress in tie-dyed outfits and many of them live in communes.

PUNCTUATING TITLES

The following titles are italicized or underlined (something underlined in a manuscript is italicized when it is printed).

books
pamphlets
collections
periodicals
newspapers
long poems
plays
films
titles of long musical works
paintings and sculptures
television shows

If the title begins with an article, and the article does not fit the syntax of the sentence in which it is used, you may delete it.

Dickens' *Tale of Two Cities* was his favorite novel.

In a sentence, don't italicize the article before a periodical title unless it begins the sentence.

The headlines of the *Post* are legendary.

Use quotation marks to punctuate the titles of the following.

articles
essays
songs
chapters
short stories
short poems
short musical pieces
television episodes

Practice

Rewrite each of these sentences. Punctuate the titles correctly.

1. Stanley loved the opera La Traviata.
2. We saw Rembrandt's painting The Jewish Bride in Amsterdam.
3. I saw a movie made from the short story Ballad of the Sad Cafe.
4. Tony's article was on the front page of the Daily News.
5. I love the Trouble with Tribbles episode of Star Trek.

USING QUOTATION MARKS

If a quotation is short—less than about eight lines, or less than two lines of poetry—you should set it off with **quotation marks.** You also use quotation marks when you write dialogue, unless you are writing a play or screenplay.

Use double quotation marks for an ordinary quotation, title, or dialogue. Use single quotation marks for a quotation or title within a quotation or within dialogue.

"Where are you going?" I asked Manuel.
"I want to hear the reading of Arista's new poem, 'Where the Swans Nest,'" he replied.

If you write a quotation of more than a paragraph, begin each new paragraph with quotation marks. Do not use end quotation marks until the quotation is finished.

"I heard a good story today," Harry said. "There was a little boy who had a dog, and the dog adored him. They were devoted to each other.
"Years went by and the boy—he's a man now—was always with the dog." He stopped to take a sip of his drink.

When you use quotation marks with other punctuation, follow these rules.

1. Put periods and commas inside the quotation marks.

"Let's go to the movies," Rita suggested.
Don shook his head. "I'm too tired."

2. Put colons and semicolons outside quotation marks.

The professor told the class to read "Byzantium"; he'd give a quiz on Monday.

3. Put question marks and exclamation points inside quotation marks when they are a part of the quotation. Put them outside quotation marks when they are a part of the whole sentence.

"Did you like the song?" Peter asked.
"It was wonderful!" Deirdre replied.
Did Peter know the folk song "If I Had a Hammer"?

Practice

Rewrite these sentences. Add quotation marks where they are needed.

1. Has everyone done the reading for today? Dr. Giannone asked.
2. Yes, the class chorused, we have.
3. Let's start with the poem The Charge of the Light Bridage, suggested the professor.
4. The professor read aloud: Half a league, half a league,/Half a league onward.
5. The class knew by heart the lines Theirs not to reason why/Theirs but to do or die.

USING SEMICOLONS, COLONS, AND DASHES

A **semicolon** indicates a pause in a sentence that is stronger than a comma's. Use a semicolon to separate the clauses in a compound sentence without a conjunction.

The sea breeze was gentle; it lulled me to sleep.

Use a semicolon between items in a series that contain commas.

I wore my long, silky skirt; a new straw hat; and a pair of clunky, high-heeled shoes.

Use a semicolon to separate the clauses in a compound sentence if the second clause begins with a conjunctive adverb such as *however, nevertheless,* or *therefore.*

I'd never vacationed in the Caribbean before; however, a friend had advised me to visit the island of Saba.

A **colon** indicates a strong break in a sentence. Use a colon to introduce a list or a long quotation.

I brought these items with me: three bottles of suntan lotion, sunglasses, two swimsuits, and snorkel gear.

Use a colon to separate two sentences when the second restates or explains the first.

I knew what I'd expected to find: there was a gentle sea lying under warm blue skies.

Use a colon to separate hours and minutes in numeral form.

I arrived on Saba at 3:45.

Use a colon after the greeting on a business letter.

Dear Sirs:

Use a colon between the city and name of publisher in a bibliographic entry.

New York: Paramount Publishers, Inc.

The **dash** indicates an interruption in a sentence that is stronger than a comma's. Use dashes to set off words or phrases that interrupt the flow of a sentence.

I never—even in my wildest dreams—expected the mountainous jungle of Saba.

Use a dash to separate a series from a summary.

Birds of paradise, parrots, and orchids—they grew wild on the island's volcanic slopes.

Practice

Rewrite this paragraph. Insert colons, semicolons, or dashes where necessary.

Charles went to a double feature movie last night *Attack of the Killer Tomatoes* and *Night of the Living Dead*. He said the first movie was really silly however, the second one was actually a little scary. The killer tomatoes actually actors in tomato suits were as absurd as they come. The plot made no sense there was something about an invasion, but he couldn't figure it out. Tonight he's going to see two others *They Saved Hitler's Brain* and *The Blob*.

USING APOSTROPHES

An **apostrophe** indicates one of two things: possession or missing letters. Use an apostrophe and *s* to form possessives with singular nouns, plural nouns that don't end in *s*, and indefinite pronouns.

The bird's nest was on the front porch.
The children's noise didn't seem to disturb the bird.
Everyone's activities just made the bird feel at home.

Use an apostrophe alone to form a possessive with a plural noun that ends in *s*.

The fledglings' chirps were a lovely sound.

If something belongs to more than one person and you list the owners, use an apostrophe and *s* only with the last noun.

We used Tom and Lynn's binoculars to watch the baby birds.

Use an apostrophe and *s* with the last word in a compound word to make it possessive.

My father-in-law's bird book identified them as finches.

When you put two words together in a contraction, use an apostrophe to indicate where the missing letters fall. Here is a list of common contractions.

I am	I'm
you are, they are	you're, they're
he is, she is, it is	he's, she's, it's
I will, you will, he will	I'll, you'll, he'll
she will, they will	she'll, they'll
I would, you would, he would,	I'd, you'd, he'd
she would, they would	she'd, they'd
I have, you have, they have	I've, you've, they've
he has, she has	he's, she's
is not	isn't
are not	aren't
was not	wasn't
will not	won't
cannot	can't
who is	who's
there is	there's
let us	let's

Use an apostrophe to indicate missing numbers in a date.

the riots of '68

Use an apostrophe and *s* to form plurals of letters, numbers, and words used as terms.

The *nay*'s have it.
There were twenty-seven *I*'s in his letter.
The date had five *8*'s.

Practice

Rewrite these sentences. Add apostrophes where needed.

1. Many of E. M. Forsters novels have been made into movies.
2. It isnt easy to get the tone of his novels right; its a filmmakers challenge.

3. Merchant and Ivorys films, including *Howards End*, are among the most successful.
4. Theyre responsible for one terrible mistake: *Maurice*.
5. Ive seen *A Room with a View* four times; its a wonderful film, and Helena Bonham-Carters performance is excellent.

USING PARENTHESES AND ELLIPSES

Parentheses are important when you want to set off a portion of a sentence, or a whole sentence, that is not vital to the meaning of the words around it. These parenthetical elements might include:

explanations: Our neighbor plies his illegal trade (lobstering) in the nearby bay.

examples: The authorities (Coast Guard and bay police) try to prevent him from lobstering there.

facts: The local shellfish contain heavy metals (especially mercury) that make them dangerous to eat.

asides or digressions: He sells the lobsters to local seafood restaurants (that's why I won't eat there).

Unless your parenthetical element is a sentence on its own, do not include end punctuation within parentheses. If a comma or period belongs after a parenthetical element, place it after the closing parenthesis.

Lobsters in our bay are not safe to eat. (Don't tell our neighbor that, though!)
People who eat at the local places don't know what they're getting (and don't get what they pay for).

You can also use parentheses around letters and numbers that indicate lists within sentences.

The most popular items in the seafood restaurants are (1) lobster, (2) shrimp, and (3) clams.

Ellipses are a series of three periods. You use them to show either a pause or trailing off of thought, or to indicate missing words in a quotation.

Here is a quotation. Below it is the same quotation, with parts deleted and ellipses used.

> "The storm was devastating to the outer islands. One or two of them just disappeared. The larger ones ended up much smaller, with houses and stores destroyed, simply swept away. Seven people were killed, and the property damage was tremendous."

> "The storm was devastating to the outer islands. . . . The larger ones ended up much smaller, with houses and stores . . . simply swept away. Seven people were killed, and the property damage was tremendous."

Note that there are four periods in the first set of ellipses. When you use ellipses after a complete sentence, you include the sentence's period plus the three ellipses marks.

Use ellipses also to indicate unfinished sentences and pauses.

> "I never knew . . ." she began, but she couldn't finish the sentence.

Practice

1. Rewrite these sentences, placing parentheses where necessary.

a. We heard the news on Thursday long after it happened, of course.

b. Three snakes a python and two boas had escaped from the zoo.

c. These snakes could eat quite a bit of supper a dog, for example.

2. Read this quotation. Then look at the rewritten version. Rewrite it, adding ellipses where portions of the quotation have been deleted.

"The escape from the local zoo of three snakes poses no real threat to the community of Black Rock. However, if you should see any of the snakes—there are two boa constrictors and a python—please notify local authorities. And if you own a small pet, such as a cat or little dog, you might want to keep it inside. The same goes for babies."

"The escape from the local zoo of three snakes poses no real threat to Black Rock. If you own a small pet you might want to keep it inside. The same goes for babies."

You now know the rules for punctuation of most kinds of sentences. You can write quotations correctly, place commas where necessary, and indicate pauses and asides. These skills will help you to communicate your ideas by writing clearly and effectively.

11

Rules of Capitalization

- **PROPER NOUNS AND ADJECTIVES**
- **TITLES OF PEOPLE AND OF WORKS**
- **SPECIAL TERMINOLOGY**
- **CAPITALIZATION PROBLEMS**

When you write, you begin every sentence with a capital letter. There are many other rules for using capital letters, though. Most writing you do, from business letters to travel articles that describe places, will require that you know the rules of capitalization.

PROPER NOUNS AND ADJECTIVES

Proper nouns name specific people, places, and things, while **common nouns** name any of a class of people, places, or things. Proper nouns should begin with a capital letter.

	Common Noun	Proper Noun
person:	woman	Susan
place:	city	Paris
thing:	holiday	Martin Luther King Day

Other types of proper nouns that you should capitalize include the following:

Organizations, companies, associations, and other institutions: Cleveland Browns, Cousteau Society, McDonald's Corporation, Airline Pilots Association, American Ballet Theatre

Nationalities and languages: French, Urdu, Iranian

Days, months, and holidays: Wednesday, November, Arbor Day, Kwaanza, High Holy Days

Government departments and organizations: State Department, Bronx County Court, Senate

Religions and religious terms: Protestantism, Jewish, Islam, Catholic, Buddha, the Koran

Historical eras: the Middle Ages, the Industrial Revolution, the Roaring Twenties

Often, a common noun becomes part of a proper noun. Then the common noun is capitalized.

Lake Michigan
Golden Gate **Bridge**

Proper adjectives are formed from proper nouns. Begin them with a capital letter.

Joycean, New Yorker

TITLES OF PEOPLE AND OF WORKS

When a title falls immediately before a name, capitalize it.

President Kennedy   General Howe
Queen Elizabeth I   John Cardinal O'Connor
Justice Rehnquist   Officer Daniels

If you are using a title alone, it is usually not capitalized, unless it is part of a formal statement.

I talked to the admiral last week.
I'd like to offer a toast to the Admiral.

Academic degrees are capitalized when they are abbreviated.

Jane Wyckoff, Ph.D.
Will Rattan, M.D.

Titles of honor are capitalized, except for *sir, my lord, my lady, his lordship,* and *her ladyship*.

Your Majesty
His Eminence

When you write the title of a book or article, capitalize the first word and all other words except for coordinating conjunctions, prepositions of five letters or fewer, articles, and the *to* in infinitives.

The Mill on the Floss
One Flew over the Cuckoo's Nest
"What to Do with Your Leftovers"

One exception to this rule is when a poem has a first line in place of a title. In that case, capitalize it as the line is capitalized in the poem.

"She took the dappled partridge"

SPECIAL TERMINOLOGY

There are many rules for the capitalization of words used in specialized writing. Some of the more general examples you might come across include the following.

Scientific terms:

Capitalize genus, lowercase species—*Homo sapiens*
Capitalize geological eras—Pleistocene epoch, Jurassic era

Capitalize names of planets, satellites, stars, constellations, and galaxies—Jupiter, the Little Dipper, the Milky Way

Military terms:

Capitalize names of armies, fleets, companies, and so on—the Continental Army, the Twenty-fourth Infantry Division, the United States Marine Corps

Capitalize names of wars and battles—the Civil War, the Spanish-American War, the Battle of the Bulge, the Battle of Gettysburg

Capitalize names of ships and aircraft—S.S. *Magellan, Challenger*, H.M.S. *Pinafore*

CAPITALIZATION PROBLEMS

Often, you will run into a capitalization question that is not answered by a specific rule. You can try looking the word in question up in a dictionary, or you can choose a reference guide to use, such as *Words into Type* or *The Chicago Manual of Style*. Here are some common problems you may face:

When you refer to a relative with a possessive pronoun—*my, his, her, their, our*—do not capitalize the title of the relationship.

Uncle Robert—his uncle Robert
Aunt Lou—our aunt Lou
Mother—my mother

When you refer to someone with a title using only the title and an article, do not capitalize the title—unless that person is the present President of the United States.

Doctor Roma—the doctor
Judge Winkler—the judge
the President—a president

When you refer to a direction, use a lowercase letter. When the same word refers to an area, use a capital letter.

the South—south of here
the Northeast—toward the northeast

When you use a plural common noun after more than one name, do not capitalize the noun.

the intersection of Main and Lewis streets

When you use a plural common noun before more than one name, capitalize the noun.

Lakes Baikal and Superior

When you spell out a hyphenated street name, do not capitalize the second number.

Forty-second Street

Certain proper nouns have fallen into common usage and are no longer capitalized. Other words that are commonly used are trademarks and must always be capitalized.

Common Usage	Trademarks
china (dishes)	Coke
venetian blinds	Xerox
brussels sprouts	Scotch tape
roman numerals	Polaroid
pasteurize	Kleenex
french fries	Bufferin

Always capitalize the word "I."

The rules of capitalization can be quirky. Follow the general guidelines in this chapter, and refer to a dictionary or reference book when you run into specific problems.

12

Word Parts and Word Meaning

- *PREFIXES AND SUFFIXES*
- *USING THE DICTIONARY AND THESAURUS*
- *DENOTATION AND CONNOTATION*

Your choice of words is part of what makes your writing unique. It's important, therefore, to use words correctly. To do so, you need to know what words mean, and you must be able to choose the right word to say what you want. You'll learn, in this chapter, how to break a word down to its component parts to determine its meaning. You'll discover, too, that definition can be flexible; there are shades of meaning in many words.

PREFIXES AND SUFFIXES

Many English words are built around *base words*. These words are like building blocks; you can add **prefixes** and **suffixes** to a base word to change its meaning or to change the word's part of speech.

A prefix is a series of letters that goes in front of the base word. Here is a chart of common prefixes.

prefix	definition	base word	new word
ante-	before	bellum	antebellum
anti-	against	war	antiwar
dis-	the opposite of	interested	disinterested
extra-	beyond	terrestrial	extraterrestrial
il-	not	logical	illogical
im-	not	possible	impossible
in-	not	active	inactive
ir-	not	rational	irrational
mid-	in the middle of	season	midseason
mis-	wrong	judge	misjudge
non-	not	standard	nonstandard
post-	after	script	postscript
pre-	before	dawn	predawn
re-	again	animate	reanimate
semi-	half, partly	conscious	semiconscious
sub-	below	tropics	subtropics
super-	more than	market	supermarket

Practice

Read these sentences. Determine the meaning of each underlined word by defining its prefix.

1. The workers' trust in the management was <u>misguided</u>.
2. The management <u>reworked</u> the contract to the workers' <u>disadvantage</u>.
3. The <u>subcommittee</u> objected, but they were ignored.
4. When they complained, the union leaders were <u>noncommittal</u>.
5. They deemed the contract <u>prolabor</u>, but they were <u>misinformed</u>.

A suffix is placed at the end of a base word. It can change the base word's part of speech, and it can also change the spelling of the base word. Here is a chart of common suffixes.

suffix	definition	base word	new word
-able	able to	excuse	excusable
-ance	condition of	rely	reliance
-ant	doing or showing	vigil	vigilant
-en	consisting of, like	wood	wooden
-ence	state or condition	depend	dependence
-ent	doing or showing	ascend	ascendent
-er	that which, one who	teach	teacher
-ful	full of	joy	joyful
-hood	state or condition	child	childhood
-ible	able to	force	forcible
-ish	relating to	fool	foolish
-ist	one who practices	violin	violinist
-less	without	hope	hopeless
-like	like	snake	snakelike
-ly	every, like	day	daily
-ment	condition of	enjoy	enjoyment
-ness	state or condition of	lively	liveliness
-or	one who	sail	sailor
-ship	state of being	relation	relationship

Practice

Read these sentences. Define each underlined word by defining its suffix.

1. The team was involved in a <u>childish argument</u>.
2. The <u>pitcher</u> had hit the <u>batter</u> with a <u>careless</u> and <u>forceful</u> pitch.
3. The umpire tried to keep the confrontation <u>peaceful</u>.

4. Both teams—the whole <u>membership</u>—rushed in defiance onto the field.
5. The fight was <u>inexcusable</u>, and the <u>commissioner</u>'s angry response was completely <u>understandable</u>.

USING THE DICTIONARY AND THESAURUS

When you want to find the right word to use in your writing, you can try using two very helpful types of reference works. A **dictionary** will help you to do several things.

1. It will show you how to pronounce a word, using phonetic symbols. These are explained in the front of the dictionary.
2. It will tell you the word's part of speech.
3. It will define the word, giving all of its meanings if it has multiple definitions. Sometimes the definition includes example sentences.
4. It may give information about the word's origin, or *etymology,* and will tell you any special ways the word might be used.

A **thesaurus** is helpful if you know what you want to say, but you want to use a stronger or more unusual word to say it. A thesaurus includes **synonyms**—words that are similar in meaning—and **antonyms**—words that are opposite in meaning. Some thesauruses are organized like dictionaries, using alphabetical order. You just look up the word and find its synonyms and antonyms. Other thesauruses are organized by category. You look up the specific word in the index. Listed under each word are the categories in which it is listed. Find the category that best matches the meaning you want, and look for a synonym or antonym under that heading.

Practice

Look up each of the words below in a dictionary. Use each word in a sentence for each definition given. Then look up the words in a thesaurus. Write down two synonyms and two antonyms for each word.

1. base
2. image
3. revolt
4. imitation
5. truncate

DENOTATION AND CONNOTATION

When you look up a word in a dictionary, you find its **denotation**—that is, its definition. However, words can evoke emotions and feelings, both positive and negative, as well. The emotions and feelings that are attached to a specific word make up its **connotation.**

It is important to consider connotations as you write. Choosing a given word over another affects the tone and mood of your writing. For example, the words "cheap" and "inexpensive" are synonyms. Their meanings are similar, but their connotations are different. What do you think of when you hear each word?

cheap—shabby, poor, down-at-the-heels, badly made, flimsy
inexpensive—a bargain, marked down, not overpriced

Notice how these sentences differ although the underlined words are synonyms.

Jeanne's date was very <u>polite</u>.
Jeanne's date was very <u>suave</u>.

Tanya was too <u>headstrong</u> for her own good.
Tanya was too <u>stubborn</u> for her own good.

The travelers were stopped by a <u>thief</u>.
The travelers were stopped by a <u>bandit</u>.

Practice

Write a sentence for each of these words. Try to make your sentences reflect the differences in each pair's connotations.

1. rough, rugged
2. robe, dressing-gown
3. patient, long-suffering
4. hug, caress
5. anger, wrath

Now you know how to find the precise meanings of words, and you can choose the word that has the meaning most appropriate for what you want to say. You know how to use the dictionary and thesaurus to improve and increase your vocabulary. All that's left is to learn how to spell the words correctly!

13

Rules of Spelling

- *SPELLING HINTS AND RULES*
- *ESPECIALLY DIFFICULT WORDS*

When you write, it is important to spell words correctly. Misspellings look sloppy, as if you don't really know the words you're using—or don't care enough to look them up. Even if you have a spelling checker on your computer, there will be words that are not in its dictionary, or which are correctly spelled but typed in the wrong place (a spell check won't catch *form* instead of *from,* for example). Once you learn the basic rules of spelling, you'll be able to improve your spelling skills.

SPELLING HINTS AND RULES

There are several helpful hints that you can use to improve your spelling. The first and most important is to use the dictionary. (For more information on using the dictionary, see pages 152–153.) You can also try to develop *mnemonic devices,* or memory aids. For example, if you can't tell *stationery* from *stationary,* remember that *stationery* is what you use to write a *letter*—both words contain an *er*.

To be sure you can spell a difficult word correctly, follow these steps.

1. Look carefully at the word. Try to memorize it.
2. Say the word aloud. Be sure you pronounce it correctly.
3. Write the word from memory.
4. Check your written word against the original.

Spelling with Suffixes

Final *e:* If a suffix begins with a vowel, drop the base word's final *e.* If a suffix begins with a consonant, keep the base word's final *e.*

care + ful = careful
believe + able = believable

There are a few exceptions to this rule, including *argument, judgment,* and *truly.*

Final *y:* If the final *y* in a base word is preceded by a consonant, change the *y* to *i* before adding a suffix—unless the suffix begins with an *i.* If the final *y* is preceded by a vowel, the *y* usually does not change.

rely + ance = reliance
rely = ing = relying
annoy + ance = annoyance

Doubling final consonants: For one-syllable words, if the word ends in a consonant that is preceded by a vowel, then you double the final consonant when adding a suffix. For two-syllable words, do not double the final consonant unless the last syllable is stressed.

chat + ed = chatted
fun + y = funny
prefer + ed = preferred
prefer + able = preferable

Spelling with ie and ei

That old rule, "*I* before *e* except after *c*," generally holds true. The exceptions are when the vowels sound like a long *a*. Then the word is spelled with *ei*.

y*ie*ld
rec*ei*ve
n*ei*ghbor

There are a few exceptions to this rule. They include *either* and *neither*, *seize*, *leisure*, and *weird*.

Another common spelling difficulty comes with words that end with *-cede*, *-ceed*, and *sede*. You must memorize these words.

Three words end in *-ceed:* exceed, proceed, succeed.
One word ends in *-sede:* supersede.
All other words with this sound end in *-cede*.

ESPECIALLY DIFFICULT WORDS

There are some words that give almost everyone problems. Many of these are *homophones*—words that sound alike but are spelled differently. Here is a list of difficult words and their definitions. Add your own problem words to this list.

advise: to give helpful information
advice: helpful information

allusion: an indirect reference
illusion: a vision of something unreal

ascent: a climb
assent: approval

altogether: completely
all together: in a group

council: a governing body, or meeting thereof
counsel: to give advice

dye: to color
die: to pass away or expire

desert: a hot, arid area
dessert: a sweet, usually following a meal

devise: to plan
device: an implement

elicit: to bring or draw out
illicit: illegal or immoral

formally: in a proper manner
formerly: in a previous time

it's: it is
its: belonging to it

lose: to misplace
loose: not tight

moral: relating to ethical principles of right and wrong
morale: emotional condition

precede: to come before
proceed: to move onward

principal: most important, or school head
principle: a basic belief

right: correct
write: to mark on paper
rite: a ceremony

sight: vision, or to look along something, such as a rifle
site: place

stationary: standing still
stationery: writing paper

their: belonging to them
they're: they are
there: at that place

to: toward
too: also
two: one more than one

weather: meteorological conditions
whether: if

whose: belonging to whom
who's: who is

your: belonging to you
you're: you are

Practice

Choose the correct word from each pair to complete the sentence.

1. The company had to cross seventy miles of (dessert, desert).
2. The leaders met in a serious (council, counsel) to discuss (their, they're) chances.

3. They decided to begin the (assent, ascent) (all together, altogether).
4. They (preceded, proceeded) through the sandy waste with high (morale, moral).
5. If the (weather, whether) stayed fair, they would be all (rite, right, write).

To know spelling is to be in control of your writing. When you know what words to use, and you use them correctly, your readers won't find themselves confused because of misspellings. Remember—when in doubt, find a dictionary.

14

Abbreviations and Numbers

- *USING ABBREVIATIONS*
- *USING NUMBERS*

There are special rules of capitalization and punctuation that go with using abbreviations. There are also rules about using numbers that tell you when to write them in word form and when to use numerals.

USING ABBREVIATIONS

An **abbreviation** is a shortened form of a word or a phrase. These are a few abbreviations you will use under almost any circumstances.

A.M.—before noon
P.M.—after noon

Use these with specific times written in numerals: 8:17 A.M.; 4:45 P.M.

B.C.—before Christ. Place after a date: 343 B.C.

A.D— *Anno Domini,* or after Christ. Place before a date: A.D. 1774

Some commonly used name, title, and degree abbreviations include:

Dr. Mr. Ms. Mrs. M.D. Ph.D.
Jr. Sr. M.A. J.D. MSW

Use these with specific names, though the abbreviations for scholarly degrees can be used at any time.

If you use a long phrase or name often in a work, you can insert its abbreviation in parentheses after the first usage. Then use the abbreviation afterward.

This year the Federal Emergency Management Agency (FEMA) has responded well to several major disasters. Former critics now praise FEMA for its flood and hurricane relief efforts.

You can use other common abbreviations or **acronyms**—words made by combining the first letters of an organization's name—in your writing. These include:

FBI—Federal Bureau of Investigation
CIA—Central Intelligence Agency
YMCA—Young Men's Christian Association
AT&T—American Telephone and Telegraph
CDC—Centers for Disease Control
NAACP—National Association for the Advancement of Colored People

Postal abbreviations should rarely be used in the text of a work. However, if you are addressing an envelope or preparing a bibliography, you can use these two-letter state abbreviations.

AL—Alabama	AK—Alaska	AZ—Arizona
AR—Arkansas	CA—California	CT—Connecticut
DC—District of Columbia	DE—Delaware	FL—Florida
GA—Georgia	HI—Hawaii	ID—Idaho
IL—Illinois	IN—Indiana	IA—Iowa
KS—Kansas	KY—Kentucky	LA—Louisiana
MA—Massachusetts	MD—Maryland	ME—Maine
MI—Michigan	MN—Minnesota	MO—Missouri
MS—Mississippi	MT—Montana	NB—Nebraska
NC—North Carolina	ND—North Dakota	NH—New Hampshire
NJ—New Jersey	NM—New Mexico	NV—Nevada
NY—New York	OH—Ohio	OK—Oklahoma
OR—Oregon	PA—Pennsylvania	RI—Rhode Island
SC—South Carolina	SD—South Dakota	TN—Tennessee
TX—Texas	UT—Utah	VA—Virginia
VT—Vermont	WA—Washington	WV—West Virginia
WI—Wisconsin	WY—Wyoming	

You can also use these abbreviations in a bibliography.

Rd.—Road	St.—Street	Blvd.—Boulevard
Ave.—Avenue	Hwy.—Highway	Pkwy.—Parkway

These abbreviations for days and months can go in your bibliography or in lists or charts.

Mon.—Monday	Tues.—Tuesday	Wed.—Wednesday
Thurs.—Thursday	Fri.—Friday	Sat.—Saturday
Sun.—Sunday	Jan.—January	Feb.—February
Mar.—March	Aug.—August	Sept.—September
Oct.—October	Nov.—November	Dec.—December

Use abbreviations in company or organization names only when they are part of the name itself.

wrong: Harper-Collins book co.
right: Macmillan, Inc.

Practice

Correct these sentences by writing out the abbreviations that don't belong.

1. James wrote a letter to the Cormel Cookie co. on Mon., Nov. 7.
2. He complained about a cookie he bought in Oct. in their shop on Hoover Blvd.
3. He ate the cookie at ll:15 A.M.; by nightfall, he needed a dr.
4. James ended up in the Cross St. Hospital from Wed. until Fri.
5. The co. wrote a letter of apology that reached James in NJ on Fri., Nov. 11.

USING NUMBERS

When you use numbers in writing, you should try to be consistent. Here are some rules to follow.

If a number can be written in one or two words, spell it out. A hyphenated number is considered to be one word.

There are nine players on a baseball team.
The crowd numbered 45,600.
Vendors sold thirty-five hundred hot dogs.

An exception to this rule occurs when more than one number is used in a passage. Then you must be consistent. If one of the numbers should be expressed in numeral form, write all of the numbers in numerals.

A record 3,620 soft drinks were purchased. This may have been because the temperature hit 95 degrees.

If a number begins a sentence, spell it out.

Three thousand four hundred tickets for the concert were sold in an hour.

If you use a number in the millions or billions, you can write the amount in numerals and spell out the words *million* or *billion*.

The sale of tickets, T-shirts, and buttons raised 120 million dollars.

You should write the following in numerals.

address numbers and zip codes: 11 Adams Street, Springfield, MA 01102
exact amounts of money (unless the amount is round and three words or fewer): $14.95; twelve dollars
decimals, percentages, and fractions: 1.4; 16 percent; 1 2/3
times of day (unless you use the word *o'clock*): 12:45; six o'-clock
dates (unless you omit the year): May 4, 1968; May fourth; the fourth of May

Practice

Rewrite these sentences so the numbers are written correctly.

1. The average price of a movie ticket today is $8.00.
2. In nineteen eighty-eight, a movie cost four dollars and eleven cents.
3. I see, on average, 90 movies a year. I saw one hundred and two last year.
4. There is something wonderfully peaceful about spending 2 hours in the dark with 100 strangers.

5. I also love buying popcorn (two twenty-five) and soda (one seventy-five).

Writing numbers and abbreviations correctly shows that you think the details of your writing are important. This can make a big impact on an editor, a professor, a coworker, or boss.

IV

The Writing Process

15

Preparing to Write

- *FINDING IDEAS*
- *NARROWING A TOPIC AND GATHERING INFORMATION*
- *ORGANIZING INFORMATION*

There is nothing more daunting than sitting down in front of a blank sheet of paper or a blank screen and finding your mind as empty as what's in front of it. Then too, there are few things more exhilarating that finding a great idea and knowing what to do with it. When you get ready to write, examine your writing ideas, choose one as your topic, and organize the information you have so that your writing task is a breeze, not a burden.

FINDING IDEAS

Ideas for writing are everywhere—in what you see each day, in what you read, hear, try, or imagine. The problem is finding an idea that suits your purpose, your audience, and the form you are using. (For more information on purpose and audience, see pages 99–101. For more information on forms of writing, see pages 11–17 and 30–38.)

To find ideas, you can use sources outside yourself, or you can use your own imagination. Here are two methods for finding ideas from outside sources.

1. Anything you read or see can be a possible source of ideas. If you are a pack-rat type who clips and saves bits of newspapers and magazines that interest you, your file of clippings is an instant resource. Did you once read an article about a German family divided by the Berlin Wall? You could write a short story about their reunion, forty years after being separated.
2. You can use what you hear, as well as see. The argument you overhear at an Indian restaurant, the discussion of work ethics between two coworkers on an elevator, the recital of marital woes one friend tells another on the bus—these are all great sources for writing ideas.

Here are four methods for finding ideas using your own imagination.

1. Sometimes, just sitting down and writing is a good way to find an idea. You can **freewrite**—write whatever comes out of your mind, just as it emerges. What results might seem at first like a page of babble, but you'll often be surprised at how your thoughts link up and provide you with ideas. Freewriting also gets you writing, and the act of writing itself can help you generate ideas.
2. One of the best places for finding writing ideas is your journal, if you keep one. There, you have recorded events, thoughts, and feelings. Anything you've written about might make a good writing topic.
3. You can use the **clustering** technique. A cluster is a visual form that helps you formulate and expand ideas. To cluster, follow these steps.

a. Begin by writing a central idea in the middle of a sheet of paper and circle it.
b. Write related ideas around your central idea. Circle them and link them to the central idea.
c. Think of ideas that connect to each related idea. Write them, circle them, and link them to the related ideas.

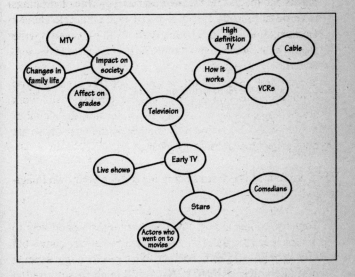

Once you've completed a cluster, you may find that it contains several ideas you can use in your writing. For example, from this cluster you may choose to write:

- an article about early stars of TV who went on to act in movies
- an editorial about how watching TV affects children's grades
- a story about an actor on one of the early live TV dramas
- a news feature about the coming of high-definition TV

4. Try asking yourself "what if" questions. These questions can open your mind to new ways of looking at things. What if, for example, a famous politician revealed that he had AIDS? Or what if a substance were discovered that allowed people to eat all they wanted without gaining weight? What if we discovered that dolphins had a complex language—and we learned to understand it? Go as far as you want with these questions.

Practice

Use freewriting, clustering, or "what if" questions to transform one of these general ideas into a specific idea for writing.

1. opera
2. mountains
3. bodybuilding
4. medicine
5. ESP

NARROWING A TOPIC AND GATHERING INFORMATION

One of the easiest mistakes you can make as a writer is to choose too broad a writing topic. An analytic essay comparing the writers Gustave Flaubert and Leo Tolstoy could go on for hundreds of pages and would probably be unfocused and confusing. A more manageable topic would be a comparison of Madame Bovary's and Anna Karenina's motives in beginning an illicit love affair.

Here are some guidelines to follow when you are narrowing and focusing your topic.

1. Consider your purpose, audience, form, and deadline, if any. Ask yourself these questions:
   What aspect of my topic will interest my audience most?
   What do I want to accomplish with my writing?
   How much time do I have to complete my writing?
   How long should my writing piece be?
   (The answers to these questions will determine the limits of your topic.)
2. Write down a general topic that interests you. Below it, list subtopics.
3. If your subtopics are still too broad, choose one as a general topic and repeat the listing process.

Here is an example of how listing can help you narrow and focus your topic.

Purpose: to entertain
Audience: general magazine readers
Form: magazine article
Deadline: one month
Length: 4-6 pages
General topic: summer vacation
 a. school's out
 b. summer road trips
 c. foreign tourists
General topic: school's out
 a. kids at home for summer
 b. summer camps
 c. teacher's time off

A good topic for an entertaining article in a magazine might be the effect on a parent's freedom of having the kids at home all summer.

Practice

Choose one of these general topics. Determine a possible audience, purpose, form, deadline, and length for a piece of writing. Then use listing to narrow and focus your topic.

1. childcare
2. the legal system
3. the 1960s
4. UFOs
5. Yugoslavia

Once you know exactly what you want to write about, you'll have to find information about your topic. Even if you are writing a fictional piece, there will most likely be information you need. If, for example, you are writing a story set in South Dakota at the turn of the century, you'll need to find out what South Dakota was like at that time, what kinds of people lived there, what they wore and ate, and what kind of work they did. The more you know about a topic, the more detailed and convincing your writing will be. Here are some ways you can gather information.

1. *Research.* You can use the library resources, as discussed in detail on pages 20–22 and 199–201.
2. Ask yourself *questions* about your topic. Try dividing the topic into smaller parts and asking questions about each part.
3. Use your powers of *observation.* Look at the world around you. Use your senses to hear, see, taste, smell, and feel things that will aid you in writing on your subject.
4. *Talk* to people. Interviewing (discussed on page 22), informal surveys, and simple discussion with friends and acquaintances about aspects of your topic can often give you valuable information to use in your writing.

Practice

Go back to the topic you chose on page 174. Then use two of the methods described—researching, questioning, observing, or talking—to gather information about it.

ORGANIZING INFORMATION

Once you have gathered enough information for your writing project, you should organize it in a way that will make writing easier. There are several ways to organize information.

One method is to organize by *main idea and details* and create an **outline**. This works best for writing such as research reports, news articles, and critical or analytical essays. An outline is a rough sketch of the main points you want to cover. It doesn't usually have a lot of detail; it allows you to set out the structure of your thoughts and make sure that they follow logically. The outline is really the skeleton of your writing; once the structure is in place, all you need to do is flesh it out with the details.

Keep in mind that your outline is not carved in stone. You may find as you do your research, for example, that you've left out some key ideas or information; just add it. Make sure that the structure still works, however, and be prepared to revise. A good outline will help you pinpoint the gaps in your thinking or notes.

To write an outline, arrange your notes in groups, by subject. Each group of notes will fall under a main heading, which in an outline is indicated with a roman numeral. Beneath each main heading, and indented, you will create subheadings from the information in your notes. Mark each subheading with a capital letter. You may also include sub-subheadings, which further organize and detail your subheadings. Mark these with Arabic numbers.

Here is a sample outline for a research report on family life in early colonial days.

I. The Home
    A. housing
        1. buildings
        2. furniture
    B. clothing
        1. making clothes
        2. clothing styles
II. The Household
    A. parents
        1. domestic responsibilities
        2. social obligations
    B. children
    C. servants
    D. other relatives
III. The Church
    A. Protestants
        1. church services
        2. holidays
    B. Catholics
        1. church services
        2. holidays
IV. The Town
    A. physical layout
        1. private buildings and ways
        2. public buildings and ways
    B. class structure
        1. upper class
        2. middle class
        3. lower class

Some people find it easier to organize using an *informal outline*. In an informal outline, you use numbers for your main topics and list your subtopics beneath the main topics. A section of the outline above, written informally, might look like this:

1. The Home
   housing— buildings, furniture
   clothing—making clothes, clothing styles
2. The Household
   parents—domestic responsibilities, social obligations
   children
   servants
   other relatives
3. The Church
   Protestants—church services, holidays
   Catholics—church services, holidays
4. The Town
   physical layout—private buildings and ways,
                                     public buildings and ways
   class structure—upper class, middle class, lower class

You can also organize information using **chronological order.** This method is often useful for narrative writing—personal essays, stories, and novels. Use a time line to organize events chronologically, or chart events by minutes, hours, days, weeks, month, or years.

You can use **comparison and contrast** to organize your information. This is useful in certain kinds of essays, articles, and reports. Use a chart to help you. Label the columns *Similarities* and *Differences*. Then list the ways in which the things you are comparing are alike and are different.

You can organize information by **cause and effect.** This works well for persuasive essays and articles. Use a cause-and-effect pyramid to help you. If you are writing about the effects that result from a cause, label the top point of the pyramid *Cause,* and write the cause. Below, list the effects. If you are describing the causes that lead to an effect, invert your pyramid.

Cause	Cause 1
Effect 1	Cause 2
Effect 2	Cause 3
Effect 3	Effect

You can organize your information by using **order of importance.** This method is effective when you are presenting reasons, as in certain essays and reports. You can begin with the most important reason and end with the least important, or begin with the least important and end with the most important. Use a list or a chart to help you organize this way.

Practice

For each of the writing projects below, decide which method of organization would work best: outline, chronological order, comparison and contrast, cause and effect, or order of importance.

1. a play about the discovery of a tenth planet
2. an article on the relative merits of Burger King versus McDonald's
3. an essay on the decline of the United States as a world power
4. a business report on the need for a new computer system
5. a short story about a man who could hear colors

You've discovered how to find ideas and how to investigate your ideas to come up with a topic of the right size. You can gather information, and you can organize the information you find. With these skills, you've streamlined the writing process, making it easier to focus on the next step—drafting.

16

Drafting

- *METHODS OF DRAFTING*
- *WRITER'S BLOCK*

At last, you're ready to write. You sit down at your desk or your favorite chair, or lie in bed, like Marcel Proust. You reach out for your keyboard, your pen, your pencil. What next?

METHODS OF DRAFTING

Before you actually begin to write, determine when you will be able to work most productively. There are two important things to consider. The first is, when are you most mentally alert and ready for writing? If you are a morning person, consider getting up an hour early to give yourself some writing time while you are still fresh. If you're a night owl, try giving up the eleven o'clock news and using that time to compose.

The other question to consider is: How much time can you productively and practically spend writing? If you tend to work best in an intensive, long block of time, try setting aside a whole afternoon each week just to write. If you do better work by writing for an hour a day, find that hour somewhere in your busy schedule.

When you put these two considerations together, you'll have devised a writing schedule for yourself. Stick to it. There's no point in having a schedule unless you follow it. You can't sit around waiting for the Muse to descend; she's probably busy elsewhere. You have to summon her, and the best way to do that is to start writing. Don't be completely inflexible, though; if it's a sunny 95 degrees outside and the beach beckons on your writing Saturday, you can postpone your work—but just until evening or until Sunday. A skill unexercised can wither away.

If the idea of writing makes you nervous and you're afraid of losing track of your thoughts, you may be the perfect candidate for the **quick draft.** Quick drafts work best for short pieces of writing, such as short stories or narrative essays. When you sit down to write a quick draft, have your outline and notes near at hand, but don't feel confined by them. Your aim is to get your thoughts down, to capture your ideas before they escape you.

While writing a quick draft, don't worry about your spelling, punctuation, or grammar. You can always go back and revise your work. Refer to outline or your notes whenever your thoughts become confused or you lose track of what you want to say. The important thing is to write. Quick drafting is not the same as freewriting, though. You're not writing whatever comes to mind. You've chosen your topic, found information on it, and organized the information. You have a basic blueprint to follow. Keep in mind, though, that it is *your* blueprint. If you find that your ideas go in a different direction than you had originally planned, you can change your plan to fit what you've written.

If, on the other hand, you prefer to write in a highly structured way, you can write a **slow draft.** Slow drafts are most appropriate for writing such as reports and long articles. When you write a slow draft, you refer to your notes and outline often. Write slowly, and reread and revise as you go along. Your first draft will be much closer to a final draft using this technique, but you will still need to revise and rework your writing.

Because you'll be making changes in your writing, be sure to double-space the lines and leave wide margins. That way, you have room to make notes and mark changes.

If you come to a spot in your writing where you can't think of the right word, phrase, or even sentence, leave a blank space. You can be more precise later. While drafting, you want to keep writing, not get bogged down in a search for the perfect word. If you *do* get bogged down, try going back a few paragraphs and rereading what you've written. You can often restart your momentum this way.

The important thing to remember about drafting is that your draft is always a work in progress. Nothing you write is immutable until you send it off or hand it in (and even then, an editor or teacher or boss may well make changes). If you get stuck on a chapter or a paragraph, you can change it later. If your sentences come out sounding awkward, you can revise them. A first draft is only that—the first attempt. You don't have to consider any draft a final draft until you are completely satisfied with what you've written.

WRITER'S BLOCK

Most writers have, at some time, experienced that dreadful condition called **writer's block**. When you have writer's block, you are unable to write what you want or need to write. Sometimes you can't come up with any writing ideas. Even if you have an idea, the act of writing has become impossible for you. For some writers, this happens frequently. For an unlucky few, the block can go on for days, weeks, months . . . even years. What should you do if you find you are suffering from writer's block?

1. Change your workspace. Try writing someplace completely different—in a park, in the library, in the basement. If you

can't do this, try changing the physical setup of your space—move your desk, put up a new picture. Give yourself a new view.

2. Begin your piece somewhere other than at the beginning. Write the ending first. Start in the middle. Write one scene you are sure about. It will lead to another.

3. Find a distraction. Work on something different for a while, or forego writing entirely for a short time. Watch a movie, take a drive. Let your project simmer at the back of your mind as you give yourself a break.

4. Try approaching your project from a different direction. Experiment with a new form or a different point of view. Focus on a new character.

5. Put yourself into a different role. Imagine you are writing as your professor, as one of your characters, as Virginia Woolf. Distancing yourself from your role as writer can often free you to write.

Whatever you do, don't despair. Writer's block is not fatal. It's the result of stress, or fear, or discomfort with the writing process, or a dislike of your subject. Try to determine the reason for your block. Then choose one of the approaches cited to attack the problem.

Practice

Choose one of these topics to write about. Write a first draft on the topic, using whichever drafting method you think would work best for you.

1. cable home shopping networks
2. unusual ways to save money
3. food product labeling
4. buying a new car
5. your favorite (or least favorite) talk show

So you've written something! It may look like little more than a few scribbled sheets littered with marginalia, but it's the heart of your writing project. It's not perfect, though, and perfection is what you strive for. You want that A+, that publishing contract, that promotion, that check in the mail. To get it, you'll have to revise.

17

Revising

- *REVISING THE WHOLE*
- *REVISING PARAGRAPHS*
- *REVISING SENTENCES*
- *REVISING WORDS*
- *REVISING WITH A READER*

After you've completed your first draft, you'll turn your attention to revising. Revision is a step many writers leave out—and it's one of the most important things you can do to improve your writing. It's not easy, though; it means looking at your work with an objective, critical eye.

REVISING THE WHOLE

When you've finished a draft, put it aside for a little while—a few hours, a day or two. When you go back to it, you'll be able to see it more clearly and objectively. Read it through. At this stage, you are checking to see how your thoughts and ideas hang together. Ask yourself these questions.

1. Is the form of my piece appropriate for my audience and purpose?

2. Is the tone of my piece appropriate for my topic and audience?
3. Have I included enough information or details for my readers to understand what I am trying to say?
4. Do all the details, facts, and examples in my writing relate to my main thesis or focus?
5. Will my introduction capture my readers' interest?
6. Does my conclusion provide a sense of closure?
7. Do the various parts of the work (chapters, acts, sections) blend together?

When you can answer "yes" to these questions, you have achieved unity and coherence in your work as a whole.

REVISING PARAGRAPHS

You'll have to get more specific in your revising than just looking at the broad overview. Your paragraphs must be clear. Each one should work well on its own, and they should work well together. Ask yourself these questions.

1. Does each paragraph contain a link to the main idea or focus?
2. Is each paragraph unified? Do its details and examples all relate to the main focus?
3. Is each paragraph coherent? Does each paragraph connect smoothly with the next? Have I used transitions well?
4. Are the sentences in my paragraphs in the best and most logical order?

When the answer to all of these questions is "yes," then you've achieved unity and coherence in your paragraphs. (See pages 92–97 for more information about writing paragraphs.)

Practice

Revise this paragraph. Be sure it does not include any unnecessary details and that the sentences are in the most logical order.

The heat wave of 1993 will long be remembered in the Northeast. In Manhattan, several deaths were blamed on the heat. Cities sweltered in an ozone haze, while even the countryside hovered near the hundred degree mark. The Midwest, on the other hand, was uncustomarily cool and rainy. New York broke a heat record on three consecutive days.

REVISING SENTENCES

Each sentence in a paragraph should be as strong as possible. Your paragraphs are only as good as your sentences. When you revise sentences, you want to look for these problems.

Repetitive sentences: If all your sentences begin or are structured the same way, they will be boring. Change the beginnings. Don't use the same phrase again and again.

He watched the fishing boat drift toward shore. He noticed no one was in it.
revised: The fishing boat drifted toward shore. He noticed no one was in it.

Unvaried sentence length: If all your sentences are the same length, your writing will be dull. Too many short sentences can make writing seem choppy, but too many long ones can be confusing and annoying. Vary your sentence length.

Sometimes you can combine two weak sentences to make one strong one, or you can break one long, unwieldy sentence in two.

The fishing gear was intact. The life vest was gone.
revised: The fishing gear was intact, but the life vest was gone.

Though it was half full of water, the boat was still moving as it came near the dock and something about its movement told Tom that something was wrong and made him nervous.
revised: The boat, half full of water, moved near the dock. Something about its movement made Tom nervous.

Empty sentences: An empty sentence repeats what has already been stated or states something not supported by facts or examples. Delete these sentences, or add facts and examples to support them.

Tom was afraid. He found the empty boat frightening.
revised: Tom found the empty boat frightening.

Padded sentences: A padded sentence contains unnecessary words. Many padded sentences use the passive voice.

The boat was tied up by Tom.
revised: Tom tied up the boat.

Other padded sentences use words or phrases that can be reduced or deleted.

The fact is that the boat owner was missing.
revised: The boat owner was missing.

Tom searched the boat in order to find out what had happened.
revised: Tom searched the boat to find out what had happened.

Being that he found a bloodstain, Tom suspected foul play.
revised: Finding a bloodstain, Tom suspected foul play.

When you revise your sentences, ask yourself these questions.

1. Have I used the active voice as much as possible in my sentences?
2. Have I kept my tenses consistent?
3. Have I avoided fragments and run-on sentences?
4. Have I avoided repetition and used a variety of sentence types?
5. Have I used sentences of varied lengths?

When you can answer "yes" to all these questions, your sentences are in good shape. (See pages 67, 81–88, 115, and 117 for more information about writing sentences.)

Practice

Revise these sentences by varying the beginnings, combining, or deleting unnecessary padding.

1. Route 1 is an interesting road. Route 1 was once the main road between New York and Boston.
2. The fact is that much of Route 1 is now a Miracle Mile.
3. The road is full of fast food restaurants. It is full of minimalls.
4. Route 1 changes, however. It changes when it reaches Maine.
5. The thing is that there, it hugs the coastline and becomes very scenic.

REVISING WORDS

When your sentences are in good shape structurally, take a look at the words they contain. Your word choice makes a tremendous difference in your written work. You want to be sure to have chosen the strongest, best, and most appropriate word in every instance when there is a choice to be made. Be as varied, sharp, and specific as possible. Don't use a clichéd or overused word when you can think of a fresh one. Don't use jargon or language inappropriate for your audience. When you revise for word choice, ask yourself these questions.

1. Have I used clear, vivid language?
2. Are my words precise? Are my connotations what I intended?
3. Are my words appropriate for my audience?
4. Have I avoided clichés and unnecessary jargon?

If your answers to all these questions are "yes," your word choices are strong and well considered. (See pages 99–102, 120–123, and 153–154 for more information about word choice.)

Practice

Choose the best word from each pair for these sentences. Assume that your family is your audience.

1. The accident was (bad, terrible).
2. It (tied up, snarled) traffic for four miles.
3. The (road, access) to the bridge was closed off.
4. (Onlookers, Rubberneckers) slowed traffic in the other direction.
5. The (good, astonishing) thing was that no one was (seriously, badly) injured in the accident.

REVISING WITH A READER

You may sometimes find that you have trouble criticizing your own work. You may be so involved with what you have written that you cannot distance yourself enough to be objective. In this case, you may want to give your writing to someone else to read. Keep these pointers in mind if you do.

1. Show your writing only to someone whose literary opinion you trust.
2. Keep the reader relationship courteous. Even if the response you get is not what you'd hoped for, thank your reader.
3. Be sure you understand your reader's responses. If he or she dislikes something about your writing, find out what it is and why it displeases. Encourage your reader to be detailed in his or her response.
4. Remember that you don't have to take the advice your reader offers. You are the final judge of your writing. Even a professional editor can't force you to make a change you don't feel right about making (though they can refuse a contract if you don't!).

You've revised your work, from its broadest structure and style to the structure and style of its paragraphs and sentences to the choice of your words. Your writing is in good shape, so now it's time to proofread.

18

Proofreading

- *PROOFREADING MARKS*
- *PROOFREADING CHECKLIST*

When you have your writing in a state that basically meets with your approval, you have one more task to perform: proofreading. Proofreading cleans up the little errors in spelling, grammar, punctuation, and capitalization you may have missed while revising.

PROOFREADING MARKS

There are special marks used by professional editors, copy-editors, and proofreaders that you too can use. These marks are helpful because they show exactly what needs to be done to correct an error. Here are the proofreading marks you should know.

MARK	MEANING	EXAMPLE
∧	insert	cor∧ect
⊙	insert period	The dog barked ⊙
⌒	insert comma	Later‿the moon rose.
⌣	insert quotations	⌣ No!" she cried.
#	insert letterspace	The dog#howled.
/	make lowercase	the /Baby
≡	make uppercase	ṯimothy
⟋	delete	a big big yellow moon
⟋⟋	delete and close up	biaͦrd
⌒	close up	school ⌒house
∿	transpose	f r∿ei∿n d
◯	spell out	⑭
¶	make a paragraph	¶Five days later, we left.
.....	ignore change	The cast iron pot boiled over.
ⓢⓟ	correct spelling	propri⌢tor ⓢⓟ

Here is a sample proofread passage from a short story.

¶Karin hadnt̬ seen her sister in a decaid. ⓢⓟ delia had change̬d ≡
and not for the better‿she looked old, haggard‿worn out.
Her hare ⓢⓟ was gray‿and ⊙≡ her shoulders were bowed.∧ Delia?"
Ḵarin vens̬hured. Her mouth was dry, and the words cậme
out hⓈⓟorsely. "Is that you∧"
  Delia̬s head came up, and she smile̬. With that smile, d
the years fell‿away, and suddenly ḵarin was ⑫ again. ≡

PROOFREADING CHECKLIST

Some specialists recommend reading your piece of writing backward, word by word, when proofreading. However, this technique is really only useful for catching spelling problems. If you are a bad speller, you might try reading backward. Otherwise, read from start to finish, and watch for these problem areas. The chapter references tell you where to find more information about each area.

1. Grammar: Have you used adverbs and adjectives correctly? Do your pronouns agree with their antecedents? Do your subjects and verbs agree? Are your verb tenses correct and consistent? (Chapters 5 and 9)
2. Punctuation: Have you ended sentences with the appropriate end marks? Have you used commas correctly? Is your use of quotation marks, apostrophes, dashes, and parentheses correct? (Chapter 10)
3. Spelling: Have you followed general spelling rules? Did you check questionable words in the dictionary? (Chapters 13 and 14)
4. Capitalization: Did you start each sentence with a capital letter? Are proper nouns and adjectives capitalized? (Chapter 11)
5. Abbreviations: Have you used abbreviations only where appropriate? Have you placed periods correctly in abbreviations? (Chapter 14)
6. Numbers: Have you spelled out numbers of one or two words? Have you written other numbers correctly? (Chapter 14)

Read your work over once. Indicate changes with the proofreading marks on the previous page. Then, after taking a break, read your writing again. You'll probably find at least one or two more errors.

Practice

Read this paragraph. Use proofreading marks to indicate corrections.

Our office recently got a knew phone sistem. the new system is very complex. It inculdes such abilities as call waiting redial, and voice male. We can make confernce calls with as many as 8 people. The only problim with it is its very cimplexity. Even after a seminar on How to use them, few workers can do more then dile a number.

You now know how to go through the entire writing process. You can find an idea by freewriting or clustering. You can mold that idea into a topic and narrow the topic until it is a manageable size. You can find information on your topic and then organize the information you've collected. You can write an outline, a first draft, revise, rewrite . . . until you're satisfied. Finally, you can proofread what you've written. Your writing is complete, and as near perfect as you can make it. Congratulations!

V

Electronic Research and Computing

19

Library Research

- *LIBRARY CATALOGS*
- *SPECIALIZED INDEXES AND DATABASES*

If you are computer literate, there are many things you can do with a computer that will help you improve your writing skills. To start, you can increase your research options if you know how to use a library's computer resources.

LIBRARY CATALOGS

You learned to use the library catalog in Chapter 2. Most libraries have turned to computerized catalog systems, so knowing the best way to use computerized catalogs will help you in your research. If you know the title or author of each book you want, you won't have any problems. But what if you are looking generally for books on a specific topic?

Imagine that you want information on diaries written by women during the Civil War years. Your start-up screen on a computerized catalog might look something like this:

```
-SEARCH:
  -AUTHOR
  -TITLE
```

-KEYWORD
-SUBJECT

Since you're looking for material on a broad topic, you can start with SEARCH KEYWORD or SUBJECT. Press the indicated key to begin. Then you might type in **Diaries, Civil War,** or **Journals, Civil War**. If your library has nothing under those headings, you can try **American History, Civil War** or **United States History, Civil War.** It will probably take a little experimentation to determine how the catalog is organized and what listings are used. The ease with which you locate books that will be useful depends on how specific the headings in the catalog are and how closely they match what you type in. You may have to try several different headings to find what you are seeking.

Your library's computer catalog may be linked to those of other area libraries. In that case, the books listed may be held at libraries other than your own. The computer will give a list of the included libraries and can explain the abbreviations for each library's name. Then you can tell by the listing where each book is held. Even if a book is owned by another library and not yours, you can usually ask that it be sent to your library for your use. Better systems will include shelf location, whether a given book is checked out and if so, the date due. Some systems also allow one to recall a checked-out item.

Practice

Choose one of the topics below. Use a computerized catalog to conduct a search for two or three books on your topic. Try several different listings to find books.

1. London's Great Fire of 1888
2. causes of the French and Indian War
3. the Watergate break-in

4. the films of Alfred Hitchcock
5. building New York's subway system

SPECIALIZED INDEXES AND DATABASES

Most libraries, especially big public libraries and university libraries, contain computerized indexes. Often, they have the *Readers' Guide to Periodical Literature* on computer. (See page 21 for more information about using the *Readers' Guide*.) Another computerized index is called *InfoTrak*. It includes nearly one thousand periodicals. If you are looking for an article on a particular topic, you can look up your topic in *InfoTrak* and the index will list which periodicals have covered your topic in the last four years. *InfoTrak* also carries the full text of six months of the *Wall Street Journal* and sixty days of the *New York Times*.

Another helpful computerized index is the *Government Publications Index*. This index lists materials published by the government and listed in the Printing Office's monthly catalog.

The *Legaltrac Database* lists nearly eight hundred legal publications, from 1980 to the present.

One of the most useful online services you may use is called DIALOG. DIALOG contains nearly 300 databases, with indexes and information on topics such as business and industry, sciences, education, social sciences, law and government, news, and famous people. You can use it to look up book reviews, see the Philosopher's Index, and find information on fisheries in the United States. It also contains a magazine index similar to that of the *Reader's Guide*.

Other major database services include the Knowledge Index, which is the DIALOG system for use after business hours. Its cost is lower, but it includes only about one-tenth of the regular DIALOG databases. There is also Nexis/Lexis, which includes the *New York Times*, *Newsweek*, and fifty other magazines, wire services, information on banking and stocks, and a huge law database. ORBIT includes nearly seventy databases on science and technology. NewsNet is a service containing over 300 industry newsletters.

Some of these services also offer special information for writers or other groups. Called Special Interest Groups or SIGs, these databases are aimed toward their particular group's interests. They may offer conferences with writers and editors and networking opportunities with writing professionals.

To find databases on other topics, there are several directories you can consult. One is the *Directory of Online Databases,* published by Ciadra/Elsevier. There is also the *Database Directory,* published by Knowledge Industry Publications. These are available through subscription and can also be found in some libraries.

You don't have to use DIALOG or other online services in the library. If you have a *modem,* you can gain access to these services from your home. (See page 209 for more information on modems.) If you use one of these databases in a library, you may be able to do so for free or a lower charge. However, when you use them at home, you will be charged an hourly fee that can be quite expensive.

To search for a topic in an online service such as DIALOG, follow these steps.

1. Choose the database source that you need.
2. Type in a topic or a group of linked topics. You can combine topics with the words *and, or,* or *not. And* links two topics together, while *or* and *not* exclude topics or aspects of topics. For example, if you were researching attempts at escape over the Berlin Wall, you might type in *Berlin Wall* and *escape* and link these two descriptors with *and.* The database would show you only the files that cover both topics.
3. Ask the computer to download the index's list of citations, if

the list is short enough. If the list is still long, continue to shorten it by adding descriptors. You could limit your search further by typing in *Berlin Wall and (escape or protest)*.

4. Look through the list of citations to see a) which are most useful for your research needs and b) which are available at your library.

One of the most important innovations in computer research is called *CD-ROM,* or Compact Disk Read-Only Memory. CD-ROM uses a compact disk similar to the ones you might listen to on audio equipment. However, this CD can be read on a computer. Reference works, including whole sets of encyclopedias, can be stored on CD-ROMs. With the right hardware and software, you can research topics at very high speed. The technology is now mature, so the cost of the CDs, the CD-ROM players, and the interfaces are fairly reasonable and there are many brands from which to choose.

Another research option is the Electronic Newsstand, an on-line service begun in 1993 offering magazines to Internet users. As of this writing, the service includes ten magazines, including the *National Review,* the *New Yorker,* the *Journal of NIH Research,* the *New Republic,* and the *Economist.*

Practice

If you have access to a database index, use it to find information on one of these topics.

1. the results of the latest eruption of Mt. Pinatubo
2. reviews of Toni Morrison's latest novel
3. teaching animals to understand human language
4. treatments for autism
5. special effects in Steven Spielberg's *Jurassic Park*

You've now increased your research capabilities by learning how to use a computerized library catalog and how to tap into online databases. This puts you ahead of everyone who is still thumbing through the *Reader's Guide to Periodical Literature;* you have many more options than they do.

20

Hardware

- *THE COMPUTER*
- *THE PRINTER*
- *THE EXTRAS*

What you write with is becoming more important every day. A computer or word processor gives you capabilities you don't have with an ordinary typewriter. If you don't have one, you'll want at least to consider getting one. If you're still writing on paper with a pen or typewriter, consider how much time you lose to rewriting your material in a form others can use. Try keeping a diary of how much time it takes; you may be surprised. Computers are no longer the wave of the future—they're the present, especially for writers.

THE COMPUTER

As a writer, you'll be most concerned with the word processing capabilities of your computer. You can buy a word processing system that does nothing else, but in doing so you limit yourself severely. A computer gives you the option to do many things that can aid your writing, such as adding on specialized software, inserting graphics, and conducting online research. It also makes it much easier for you to exchange information and communicate with others.

Your first decision is: do you want a desktop computer, or a notebook? A desktop computer is cheaper, and the components are usually more comfortable to work with; however, you can't take it with you. Almost everything connected with a notebook is more expensive, and there are certain practical concerns that don't arise with a desktop model: battery life, cramped keyboard, relatively poor screen resolution, and security/safety issues (damage or theft are more likely). But, you can take it just about anywhere; current models weigh between 4–6 pounds (not counting batteries), and for many commuters and travellers, this portability is a huge advantage.

Your computer will include a **keyboard,** on which you type your words and your commands. The size and position of keys on your keyboard is a matter of personal preference. Desktop computers offer full-size keyboards; notebook models are generally condensed. If you are used to touch typing, you'll find standard keyboard layout easy to use. There are alternate keyboard layouts available, however, and these can increase your typing speed considerably. Your keyboard will have control and function keys, which you press along with other keys to initiate special functions and control the movement of the cursor on your screen.

You will also find a **mouse.** This is a box with a roller that you move on your desktop. It moves the cursor on your screen correspondingly. If you aren't entirely comfortable with a keyboard, you might be happier using a mouse. You'll still have to do your writing on the keyboard, but you can issue commands with your mouse. Mice are now standard with most computers, such as the Macintosh, or IBM-compatibles that support Windows. With others, they can be added on. Notebook computers have various methods for mimicking a mouse; some use a trackball, others a button in the middle of the keyboard, and others have a mini-mouse pull out from the side.

You'll also have a **monitor,** or a screen. These come in different sizes, with different degrees of resolution, or clarity. You can get them in color or greyscale monochrome. Your monitor's size, resolution, and color is also a matter of personal preference (and budget). Notebook monitors have improved greatly, but their resolution is still not generally as sharp as most desktop models. This becomes a factor if you use your machine a lot, as poor screen resolution often leads to fatigue and eyestrain.

Your computer will have **disk drives.** You'll need a hard disk drive, which enables you to store and use a great deal of information and to work with it quickly. You will also have a floppy disk drive, which allows you to add software to your hard disk or computer and can also help in moving data around. Some older computers operate with two floppy drives instead of one hard and one floppy.

Nowadays, a computer's memory is most often measured in **megabytes,** or MB. One megabyte equals 1024 kilobytes, and a kilobyte equals 1024 bytes, or 1024 characters and spaces. Get as many megabytes as you can afford, and be ready to add on memory as you need it. You'll always seem to need more.

Your hard drive's storage capacity is also measured in megabytes. A 250-megabyte hard drive is about the smallest available new, as of this writing. However, if you're buying an older or used system, smaller drives will be available.

THE PRINTER

There are several types of printers available. If you're in the market for a brand-new machine, about the only kinds of machine are laser printers and ink-jets. If, however, you're looking at the secondhand market, many older types are still available. You'll probably want to buy the best printer you can, especially if you'll be sending your writing to editors and publishers.

Daisy-wheel printers work like daisy-wheel typewriters. They are slow and loud, and are relatively expensive. However, they produce manuscripts that look like they were typewritten, and you can easily change the print font. However, if you will be using lots of italics, you will have to change the wheel every time. You will probably grow weary of this quickly.

A **dot-matrix printer** prints in a series of minuscule dots. These printers are relatively inexpensive. The quality of their resolution varies, and they can be very loud and slow.

An **ink-jet printer** produces near letter-quality work. These printers are very quiet and pretty fast, and many can use regular letter paper. However, the ink cartridges can be quite expensive, and the ink will smear if touched while wet. The output can also be fuzzy, due to ink being absorbed into the paper.

A **laser printer** is a top-of-the-line machine. Laser printers electronically attach letters and images to paper. Their quality is very high, but so is their price. They are very fast and very quiet, and can reproduce graphics well. If you're going to be doing lots of graphics, be sure your laser printer has PostScript (a computer language used for imaging).

Thermal printers produce poor quality type and require special paper, like a fax. They are quite inexpensive, but nearly obsolete; check carefully to see if you can still get servicing.

Some printers offer special features. Among the features you might find important are the following.

1. *Multiple fonts:* Laser printers and some ink-jets offer many fonts. Daisy wheels do too, but they require changing of the wheel.
2. *Color printing:* Many laser printers offer this, but it may be unnecessary unless you're doing serious desktop publishing.
3. *Superscript/subscript:* If you do a lot of work with footnotes

or mathematical terminology, you might find this capability useful.

Your printer will take paper by the sheet, by fanfold, or in a continuous roll (only thermal printers use rolls). Many dot-matrix printers offer have sheet feeders as optional components. Continuous paper has the disadvantage of an extra strip of perforated paper at each side, which you must tear off. Sheet-fed printers can use different types of paper.

THE EXTRAS

Once you've purchased the basics, you have some options. A **modem** is an option that is becoming more and more useful and widespread. Modems link computers by way of the telephone. Some computers come with internal modems; with others, you add on the modem as an external piece of hardware. With a modem, you can tap into research databases from your home. You can also receive and send electronic mail, or e-mail, which enables you to transmit and receive documents instantly. E-mail is often better than a fax, because you can edit the text.

You can also buy **cards,** or **boards,** for your computer. These increase the computer's capabilities in various ways. On the cards are printed circuits and components that are coded to perform particular tasks. If your computer is able to accept cards, they can add memory or link the computer to a printer, a modem, or a CD-ROM player.

Some experts say that the wave of the future in computers is the **voice synthesizer,** which allows the computer to speak and to respond to spoken commands. Voice recognition is still in its infancy, but it has been used for years. At the moment, this option is probably only useful for the vision-impaired writer. (It does come standard on audiovisual Macintoshes.)

You've got your hardware: the actual pieces of your computer that you need to write, transmit, and print. You have the capability to do all sorts of tasks that weren't even possible a decade or two ago. Now it's time to choose exactly what you want your computer to do.

21

Software

• WORD PROCESSING PROGRAMS
• OTHER SOFTWARE

Once you have the hardware you need, you'll want to choose
software that will help you with your particular writing needs.
There are dozens of programs out there. How can you choose
one that will work well for you?

WORD PROCESSING PROGRAMS

Your software enables you to use your computer for writing
and editing. There are many word processing programs available, and each one offers slightly different options. One way to
determine what program will be useful to you is to read software reviews in magazines. Another is to ask around. Find out
what other writers you know use. Ask them why they use it, and
about any problems they may have had. Find out what special
capabilities their programs have, and what they especially like
about them.

You can also ask experts, people who work in computer or
software stores. Be prepared to tell them exactly what you want
in a word processing program. They should be able to advise

you about how each program measures up to your wants and needs. Ask these questions.

1. Does the software match your hardware? There's no point in buying software that your computer can't use.
2. Is the program relatively easy to learn? If you're a novice, you might find some programs difficult. Look over the manual for any program you're considering. Will you have the patience to learn to use it?
3. Is the program easy to use? Once you've learned the basics, will you be able to do what you need to do quickly and efficiently?
4. Does the program address your particular needs?

While there are a great many programs out, WordPerfect and Microsoft Word are the current leaders (Nisus Writer, for the Macintosh, is also a good choice). These programs offer many features, but, most important, they allow you to exchange files and information with others easily, since a) they are so widely used and b) they offer the ability to convert from many other, older formats. Buying lesser known programs may seem cheaper, but it will probably give you some real headaches down the road.

You can expect to find word processing basics (such as creating and saving files, simple formatting, and spell checking) on any program offered nowadays. Some of the more interesting and less standardized features now available include:

-Automatic footnotes
-Automatic table of contents
-Multilanguage spell check capability
-Style sheets
-Thesaurus
-Tables
-Outlines

-Mail merge
-Sorting

OTHER SOFTWARE

You can increase the capabilities of your word processing program by adding other software to your computer. For example, you can buy a **textual analysis program** (if it is not already included in your word processing software). These note problems in grammar, punctuation, and style that vary from the rules the program includes. They will note punctuation lapses, passive verb use, sentence fragments and run-ons, and repetition. However, they are very basic and must be configured for individual style. If Marcel Proust had used one, it would have informed him his sentences were too long; Hemingway would have learned his were too short. e.e. cummings would have had endless trouble with the capitalization rules. You'll probably create more problems for yourself using a textual analysis program than you'll solve.

A **thesaurus** can be a useful add-on (again, if not already included). If you have trouble with word choice, an electronic thesaurus can help you find stronger words. However, a thesaurus uses a lot of memory. Be sure your computer can support it.

You can purchase electronic **notepads,** which allow you to make notes as you think of them, quickly and efficiently. Along the same lines are electronic **calendars** and **phone books,** on which you can note appointments, names, and numbers. These are useful because, as long as they are compatible with your equipment, you can simply transfer new files to your regular computer, without wasting time and effort recopying or retyping.

There are many programs that can instruct you in writing skills. These teach everything from composition to business writing, from fiction writing to using figurative language. You can improve your vocabulary with these programs, learn to spell better, and develop your prewriting skills. To choose an appropriate program, determine your needs, find out what's available, and match the program to your hardware.

Whatever programs you wind up using, you must learn to **back up** your files often. This just means keeping up-to-date copies of all your files on separate disks, or, if you have a lot of material, on a tape backup system. This is absolutely crucial if you have a notebook computer (what if you've just written the Great American Novel, it's all on your hard drive, and someone steals your machine?), but it is extremely important for desktop users as well. Power surges and blackouts happen; fuses blow; disks or hard drives can fail. You may also want to save a copy of any file before making major changes to it, in case you later change your mind about your edits.

Make it a habit to back up your files regularly, and keep your backups in a safe place. This should be somewhere other than in your office or desk (thieves often take anything that even looks computer-related, such as disks, while a fire or flood could wipe out anything kept in the same room). If you're backed up properly, such problems needn't become disasters.

Now you have an idea of what kind of software will be useful for your writing needs and will best suit your computer. You'll have to learn to use your software in the most efficient way, and that can be a challenging process. You'll find, though, that once you know your program, the writing process will become easier, faster, and more fun.

22

Computer Prewriting and Writing

- *PREWRITING*
- *WRITING*

Almost anything you can do on a typewriter or with a pen and paper, you can do on a computer —only faster. A computer can be a remarkable tool for prewriting and drafting, once you know how to use it.

PREWRITING

You can use the prewriting techniques you learned in Chapter 15 to help you find and organize ideas on the computer. While clustering doesn't really work well on a computer unless you have a pretty advanced graphics program, freewriting is a technique that is especially well suited to computer work. When you freewrite on a computer you can follow these steps.

1. Write freely for a short time to find and explore ideas.
2. Reread what you have written.

3. Use your block function to highlight and delete ideas you don't want to use.
4. Reread what remains. Use your block function to move ideas so that linked ideas are together.

You can also use questioning techniques very effectively on a computer. Follow these steps.

1. Input your questions.
2. Answer each question as you find information on your topic.
3. Reread what you have written.
4. Highlight and move your most useful answers together.

Once you've explored your ideas to find and limit a topic, save your prewriting file. You may find later that your writing idea isn't feasible or needs expanding. If so, you'll be able to retrieve your prewriting file and go over it again to find new ideas or add to what you have.

Organizing information on a computer is simple. Just open a new file for organizing your ideas. Then you can look at your prewriting file in a window or on the screen as you work. Whether you organize by main ideas and details, chronological order, comparison and contrast, cause and effect, or order of importance, you can use the functions of your word processing program to make the job easier. Since you can move text on a computer, you can change the order of your information and insert new information without much effort. Some word processing programs even offer outlining functions, so that they keep track of the numbering while you concentrate on the information.

Practice

Try freewriting on the computer on one of these topics. Write for ten minutes without stopping. Then look over your freewriting. Delete and move your text until you have a series of linked thoughts that make up a workable writing idea.

1. sports medicine
2. immigration quotas
3. cellular phones
4. zoos
5. recycling programs

WRITING

Drafting on a computer is very similar to other modes of drafting. However, if you have an outline, you can look at your organizational notes at the same time you are drafting. If you come to a place where your organization doesn't seem to work, you can revise your notes onscreen. If you get stuck, you can skip to another part of your draft. It's easy to fill in blanks on a computer. Remember, as in other methods, when you draft on a computer your aim is to write your thoughts down. You can revise later.

Here are some shortcuts you can use when drafting on a computer.

1. **Search:** You can use this function if you are missing necessary information. Choose a marker that will set off any notes you write to yourself; for example, a double asterisk (**).
   Place this marker before missing information and type in a brief reminder to yourself:

   The number of domestic airline flights last year was **find number.

   Then, when you are finished drafting, you can search your text for the double asterisks and fill in your missing information.

2. **Search and replace:** You can use this technique for long words or phrases that you use frequently. Create an abbreviation or marker for each one. When you are ready, search out each marker and replace each with the correct word or phrase. Be sure to use a non-English text string, e.g. "JJ," so you don't get mixed up finding real words in your text.

3. **Macros:** A macro can substitute for a block of text or for commands that you use regularly. When you are ready to insert your macro, you press a particular key or key combination. Your program will automatically insert the text or command you have set up in your macro.

Practice

Check to see if your word processing program allows you to create macros. (Read your manual, or use the Help function.) Your goal will be to create a macro for your home address. You will then be able to use the macro whenever you want to write your address—on envelopes or letters, for example. If there are other addresses you use frequently, you may want to create additional macros for them.

You've now seen how much easier it is to prewrite and write on the computer than on a typewriter or by hand. The next step moves you even farther into the computer age—revising.

23

Revising and Proofreading

- *REVISING*
- *PROOFREADING*

Your computer really shows its worth when it comes to making changes in your draft. You can move text with ease; insert and delete without retyping. After your first onscreen revision, you'll be an instant convert.

REVISING

Your style of onscreen revision depends on what is most comfortable for you. Some writers do all their revision work on the computer screen. Others print out a hard copy of their writing, mark changes on it, and then make their changes onscreen. Still others combine the two. One thing you should always do before beginning any revisions, however, is to make a copy of your draft. That way, if you delete something you later want to reinsert or make a change you want to undo, you'll have the original at your disposal.

There are four main functions you'll use when revising. These are:

1. insert
2. delete
3. move
4. search/search and replace

Here's how you might use each function when facing basic revisions.

The Entire Piece

1. Incorrect tone: **Delete** inappropriate words and phrases. **Insert** new words and phrases. **Search and replace** inappropriate words or overused phrases.
2. Insufficient information or details: **Insert** new information or details.
3. Unrelated details, facts, and examples: **Delete** unrelated material.
4. Uninteresting introduction: **Delete** dull words and phrases. **Insert** vivid words and phrases.
5. Inadequate conclusion: **Insert** new information or details.
6. Incoherent whole: **Move** paragraphs to more logical order.

Paragraphs

1. Paragraphs that are not unified: **Delete or move** details and examples that do not relate to the main focus.
2. Paragraphs that are not coherent: **Insert** transitions; **move** paragraphs that are not in a logical order.

Sentences

1. Illogical order of sentences: **Move** sentences to create a better order.

2. Passive voice: **Delete** passive verbs; **insert** active verbs.
3. Inconsistent tenses: **Delete** mistakes; **insert** new verbs.
4. Repetition: **Delete** repetitive words and phrases; **insert** new words and phrases. **Search** for repeated words.
5. Unvaried sentences: **Insert** new sentence beginnings; **move** sentence parts for variety.

Words

1. Dull language: **Delete** boring words; **insert** vivid ones.
2. Imprecise words: **Delete** words that have fuzzy meanings or connotations; **insert** new ones. You can use your thesaurus capability, if you have one, to help you find new words.

You might find a program that includes a word counter useful, especially if you customarily write very short or very long sentences. You can use it to count the number of words in each sentence. Then you can look closely at sentences with many or few words and revise them if necessary. There are also programs that count the number of words in a paragraph, which is useful if you are prone to writing paragraphs that go on for pages.

When you have followed the guidelines for revision given in Chapter 17 and revised your text on your computer according to this chapter's hints and your program's capabilities, go over your writing again. One problem with the ease and speed of computer revision is that you often leave gaps in your logic, reasoning, or chronology. If you move a sentence or paragraph, you want to be sure that it fits in well in its new placement and that it hasn't left a hole in its old location. If you add or delete words, you need to check to be sure the resulting sentence makes sense. Also check the words surrounding a change; it's easy to delete more than you intended without realizing it, or to accidentally strike a key and add letters.

Practice

Go over the draft you wrote for Chapter 16. Revise it, using the revision hints for entire pieces, paragraphs, sentences, and words. Use all four of the functions described in this chapter to make your revisions.

PROOFREADING

As with revising, you have a choice of doing your work on your hard copy and transferring to your document onscreen, working entirely onscreen, or combining the techniques. If you have a spell check program, a large portion of your work is done almost automatically. You'll still have to check for spelling errors, though. A spell check can't tell you if you misspelled a word as another word. If you have a style program, you can use it to pick up your errors in grammar and punctuation. Keep in mind, however, that these programs don't take individual style quirks into account. Use your own judgment before accepting any change such a program suggests.

When you proofread, you'll mainly use one of these functions.

1. insert
2. delete
3. search/search and replace

Here's when you might use each function with basic proofreading problems you'll face.

1. Grammar: Change incorrect usage by **deleting** words that are wrong and **inserting** correct words.
2. Punctuation: Change mistakes in punctuation by **deleting** incorrect punctuation and **inserting** corrections. If you tend

to make a certain punctuation mistake frequently, **search** for it and **replace** the mistake with the correct punctuation.

3. Spelling: Use spell check, or **delete** misspelled words and **insert** correctly spelled words.

4. Capitalization: **Delete** incorrect capitals or lowercase letters; **insert** correct letters.

5. Abbreviations: **Insert** missing periods. **Search** for frequently used incorrect abbreviations; **replace** with correct words or spelled out terms.

6. Numbers: **Search** for numbers written incorrectly; **replace** with correctly written numbers, or **delete** numbers written incorrectly and **insert** corrections.

Practice

Go over the piece of writing you revised earlier. Proofread it. Check your grammar, spelling, punctuation, capitalization, and use of abbreviations and numbers. Use the three functions listed to make corrections.

As you've seen, revising and proofreading on your computer can speed up this sometimes-painful aspect of the writing process. Don't go overboard; sometimes the ease with which you can make changes might tempt you to revise a piece to death. Use your word processing capabilities wisely, and you'll find that your writing is clearer, crisper, and more engaging than ever.

24

Desktop Publishing

Most of what you write will not require the special capabilities of desktop publishing. However, if you want to produce a brochure or a flyer, write a special invitation, or make up a fancy résumé, you can use a desktop publishing program to make your work stand out. Most word processors now permit rudimentary desktop publishing work.

DESKTOP PUBLISHING

There are several desktop publishing programs available, and like most software, these are continually being updated and improved. Some of the best known include *QuarkXPress, Ventura Publisher, PageMaker,* and *FrameMaker.* Keep in mind, though, that these are professional tools; they cost hundreds of dollars and take a while to learn. They may also require a Post-Script printer. For most people, they may be overkill. If you do decide to invest the time and money in learning and using such a program, you should also be aware that most of them (*FrameMaker* is an exception) have relatively weak word-processing capabilities. Be prepared to do that sort of work in your main word processor, and then import the files to your desktop publishing program.

With these programs, you work with two main aspects of

desktop publishing: type and graphics. You have many options for each. You will be able to choose the following options for type:

1. The font, or typeface you use. These range from *serif* type-faces, with small decorative strokes at the bottom of letters, such as Times, to *sans serif* typefaces such as Helvetica, to decorative fonts such as Hobo, Stencil, or script fonts. Your typeface will influence the feel of your document.
2. Type weight, or the thickness and width of letters. Typefaces can come in Black, Bold, Light, or various other weights.
3. Type size. You measure type in *points:* there are approximately seventy-two points in an inch.
4. Alignment. You can align your document *flush left* or *flush right.* Flush means that the first or last letters on each line are lined up with the margin. You can choose *ragged alignment,* in which each line is a different length. You can *justify* your type, making each line the same length, or you can *center* it.
5. Spacing. You can space letters to change a document's look, or space words to avoid hyphenation. You can add space between lines or between paragraphs.
6. Special type devices. These include *distorted type,* which stretches or compresses letters, and *runaround type,* which can be used to surround a piece of art.

You may have several graphics options as well. These can include:

1. Illustrations. These can be clip art, included in your desktop publishing program, or art you create yourself.
2. Informational graphics. These include charts, diagrams, graphs, and maps.
3. Photographs. Advanced programs can scan photos and reproduce them on your computer. You can manipulate these

photos by moving, cutting, or magnifying their images. This requires another piece of hardware, known as a **scanner.**

With a desktop publishing program, you will have the ability to do the following:

1. Design greeting cards
2. Make signs, banners, and certificates
3. Customize letterhead and business cards
4. Create newsletters
5. Design advertisements and flyers

Clip art available for desktop publishing varies from package to package. Some include unicorns, skulls, rockets, parrots, birthday cakes, cupids, menorahs, maps . . . almost anything you could wish. You can also create elaborate borders for your documents, with double lines, lattice work, hearts, and so on.

A word of caution: if you are readying a manuscript to send out to publishers, or a paper to submit to a teacher, don't make your work unnecessarily fancy. Your piece may stand out in the recipient's mind, but the memory probably won't be a positive one. Your words, not your graphics or your presentation, should leave an impression.

Again, remember that desktop publishing programs can be quite difficult to learn. Don't buy one unless you have a real need or desire for it. Much of the work a desktop publishing program does, you can do with a good word processing program. For example, most word processing packages now allow you to format your work by choosing margin width, making columns, inserting a limited number of graphics, choosing different type fonts and sizes, and making type bold-face or italic. You'll be unlikely to need more than this unless you are running your own business or preparing a formal presentation.

Practice

Set up the first page of a newsletter on your computer. If you have a desktop publishing program, use it for your layout, type choices, and graphics. Otherwise, use your word processing program. Do as many of the following as your program allows.

1. Lay out columns of text.
2. Write headlines in a different size and typeface.
3. Include at least one graphic.
4. Write one or two articles for the newsletter.

With desktop publishing, you can produce professional-looking documents. This can be very useful to you if you are a copywriter or designer, or if you write newsletters for your business. Think carefully before you invest in such a program, though; your word processing program may fill your needs at a much lower cost.

VI

Feedback and Publication

25

Writers' Groups, Centers, Colonies, and Organizations

- *WRITERS' GROUPS*
- *WRITERS' CENTERS*
- *WRITERS' COLONIES*
- *WRITERS' ORGANIZATIONS*

Some writers do their best work in a near-vacuum: alone in a room with only their notebook or computer for company. Many others, though, find the feedback from other writers and writing teachers invaluable. If you are one of the latter—or even one of the former—consider banding together with other writers to help improve your writing skills.

WRITERS' GROUPS

Many writers belong to a **writers' group** at some point in their careers. These groups can be very informal, just a weekly or monthly meeting at someone's home where writers exchange ideas, read each others' work, and offer advice and criticism. Some writers' groups are more formal, with a published writer or writing teacher in charge of meetings and an assignment for each get-together.

The most important consideration if you are thinking of joining a writers' group is: do you trust the judgment of the other members? Visit the group a few times before you commit yourself to it. Listen to the comments the members make, watch how they interact, and ask yourself these questions.

1. Do they criticize constructively rather than destructively?
2. Do they address the problems the writer asks them to consider?
3. Do they explain their criticism adequately?
4. Do they praise as well as criticize?
5. Do they take criticism well?
6. Do you agree, for the most part, with their criticism?

If you can answer "yes" to these questions, you have probably found a good group.

When you join a writers' group, be prepared to share your work, and be sure that you are willing to let others share theirs. You have to be a helpful member of the group, both as a critic and as the recipient of criticism. For most people, allowing others to read their writing is a very difficult and personal act. You need to tread very carefully when you critique others' work: you want to be honest, but not brutal. When critiquing a writer's work, try to do the following:

1. Praise what you like in the writing.
2. Choose one or two problems on which to focus.
3. Give good reasons for your criticism.
4. Suggest remedies for the problems.
5. Be sure the writer understands your criticism.

When you are the recipient of criticism, try to do the following:

1. Ask for specific suggestions on problems you have noticed.
2. Listen carefully to what is said and take notes.
3. Ask for explanations of any criticism you do not understand.
4. Ask for suggestions to remedy problems.
5. Remember, you do not have to take others' advice. You are your last and best critic; you decide what changes you will make.

If you can follow these rules, and the rest of the group can as well, your meetings can do a lot to improve your writing skills.

Writers' workshops are somewhat more formal groups. They usually run for a specific period of time and feature a known author as lecturer or teacher. There is often a fee for inclusion. Many universities offer workshops, especially in the summer; some libraries do so too. In a workshop, ideas and criticism are exchanged as in a group, but the workshop leader guides discussion and controls criticism. If you know the leader's work and trust his or her writing judgment, you can get a lot out of a workshop.

WRITERS' CENTERS

A **writers' center** can be very helpful to you if you don't have a space available for your work or if you don't have the necessary equipment or information to write professionally. At most writers' centers you can find information on publishing, use computers and copying machines, get advice on applying for grants, go to seminars, workshops, and lectures, and receive job referrals. Many offer space in which to write, usually a cubicle with a desk and typewriter or computer. The best known center is *Poets and Writers,* at 72 Spring Street, New York, NY 10012. Others are:

The Poetry Center of the 92nd Street Y, 1395 Lexington Avenue, New York, NY 10128.

The Loft, Pratt Community Center, 66 Malcolm Avenue SE, Minneapolis, MN 55414.

The North Carolina Writers' Network, P.O. Box 954, Carrboro, NC 27510.

The Writer's Center, 7815 Old Georgetown Road, Bethesda, MD 20814.

The Writers' Room, Fifth Floor, 153 Waverly Place, New York, NY 10014.

WRITERS' COLONIES

If you've ever dreamed of living with a group of other writers, working on your own time in a tranquil setting, with most or all expenses paid, you might consider looking into a **writers' colony.** Colonies are usually rather exclusive and require a demanding, competitive application process. Some require a weekly fee or donation. In return, you are given a space in which to work and living quarters, all in an environment of creativity where ideas can be exchanged and experimentation is encouraged.

Some of the better-known writers' colonies are:

Fine Arts Work Center in Provincetown, Box 565, 24 Pearl Street, Provincetown, MA 02657. Provides a stipend and living quarters for writers and artists.

The MacDowell Colony, 100 High Street, Peterborough, NH 03458. Provides studio and meals for writers, composers, and artists.

Ragdale Foundation, 1260 North Green Bay Road, Lake Forest, IL 60045. Provides meals, linen, and workspace for twelve writers, composers, and artists. Charges a weekly fee.

Yaddo, Box 395, Saratoga Springs, NY 12866. Sponsors writers, artists, and composers who have already achieved some recognition in their field.

WRITERS' ORGANIZATIONS

If you are planning to become a professional writer, you've probably dreamed about the joys of setting your own hours, of working as your own boss. There is a downside to this life, however. You're on your own professionally and must negotiate your contracts, deal with recalcitrant publishers, find your best insurance deal, and figure out how to pay your taxes. Fortunately, there are several organizations that can help you organize the details of your professional life. Most of these organizations require a membership fee. Some of the best known are:

The Authors Guild, Inc., 234 West 44th Street, New York, NY 10036. The Author's Guild has over six thousand members and is able to act on their behalf in business matters. To join, a writer must have had a book published within seven years of application or three articles within one and one half years.

PEN, 568 Broadway, New York, NY 10012. PEN has centers throughout the world and assists in the exchange of ideas and the maintenance of free expression. Members must be nominated.

Editorial Freelancers' Association, 71 West 23rd Street, Suite 1504, New York, NY 10010. The EFA advises freelance writers and editors in all aspects of their professional lives. The organization sponsors classes and offers medical and dental plans. Membership is open.

International Women's Writing Guild, Box 810, Gracie Station, New York, NY 10028. The Guild offers conferences and workshops, helps find jobs for writers, and refers writers to agents.

National Writers Club, Inc., 1450 South Havana, Suite 620, Aurora, CO 80012. The NWC advises its members on professional matters and offers seminars and workshops. There are two levels of membership: associate, open to any writer, and professional, open to published or produced writers.

National Writers Union, 873 Broadway, Suite 203, New York, NY 10003. This organization is open to all writers and has many offices nationwide. It aids authors in professional matters and works for better treatment for writers.

The American Society of Journalists and Authors, 1501 Broadway, Suite 302, New York, NY 10036. The Society brings writers together and offers advice on professional matters.

Being part of a group or organization can help you as a writer. You can use feedback to improve your writing and get help and advice from other writers or from experts in your field. Check out your group carefully, though; be sure it offers you what you need.

26

Publishing Markets

- *THE APPROACH*
- *THE MARKETS*

Once you've written something you really like, you might want to try to publish it. There are certain tricks of the trade you might find useful—ways to approach publishers, and ways to find the right publishers to approach.

THE APPROACH

How you approach a publisher depends in large part on what you have written. If you've finished a book, or have a good idea for a book, you might want to look into finding an agent. An agent can be very useful because most publishers are much more willing to look at writing that is submitted to them by agents they know. Some agents specialize in certain types of writing, such as children's literature or screenwriting. Most agents require you to submit a query letter before you send your writing to them. Your query letter should briefly introduce yourself, describe your writing background, and summarize the work you want the agent to consider—all within a single page. You can also send a sample chapter, if the work is fiction, or a proposal, if the work is nonfiction. Here is a sample query letter you could send to an agent or a publisher.

42 Warner Avenue
Warwick, RI 04481
November 5, 199-

Layla Jones
President
Layla Jones Agency
441 West 72nd Street
New York, NY 10021

Dear Ms. Jones:

I am a fiction writer who has recently had short stories published in *Working Woman* (August 1992) and the *L.A. Times Magazine* (June 4, 1993). I've recently completed a novel about pilot Amelia Earhart, the woman whose plane went down decades ago and who was never seen again. In my story, Earhart is not killed but survives for years on a tiny island before making her way back to civilization. She lives anonymously in one city after another, finally deciding to reveal herself to the public that searched so long for her—but the public's reaction is not what she expects.

I enclose a sample chapter from *Earhart Sighted in Bangkok*. I hope you enjoy it and would be interested in seeing the rest of the book, which I will be happy to forward to you at your request. A self-addressed, stamped envelope is included for your reply.

Sincerely,

Karen Ng

A proposal should describe your purpose and outline your nonfiction work, chapter by chapter. It should explain why your particular work is different and better than other works on the same topic. Be sure you research other books on your topic to find out if there is a market for your book. One place to look is *Books in Print,* published by R. R. Bowker. The subject guide will tell you what else is in print on your topic. Include the following points in your proposal:

1. Reasons why your book will sell, with hard numbers if you can find them on books on similar topics
2. Information on what makes your book special, unique: why it will stand out in the market
3. Information on you as the writer: what you've written before, what makes you the best author for this book
4. Table of contents
5. First chapter

When you have sent your query to an agent, give the agent several weeks to respond. If you want your sample or proposal back, enclose an **SASE**—a stamped, self-addressed envelope. If you are the sort of person who worries that the addressee never got your work, enclose a stamped, self-addressed postcard to be returned when the agent receives your writing.

To find an agent, you can ask at the Society of Authors' Representatives at P. O. Box 650, Old Chelsea Station, New York, NY 10113, or at the Independent Literary Agents Association, 21 W. 26th Street, New York, NY 10010. Some of the better-known agents are:

Agency for the Performing Arts, Inc., 9000 Sunset Boulevard., Suite 1200, Los Angeles, CA 90069 (dramatic works only).

AMC Literary Agency, 234 Fifth Avenue, New York, NY 10001.

Curtis Brown Ltd., 10 Astor Place, New York, NY 10003.

Samuel French, Inc., 45 West 25th Street, New York, NY 10010 (drama only).

International Creative Management, 40 West 57th Street, New York, NY 10019.

Russell & Volkening, Inc., 50 West 29th Street, New York, NY 10001.

Sherry Robb Literary Properties, 7250 Beverly Boulevard, Suite 102, Los Angeles, CA 90036.

Writer's House, Inc., 21 West 26th Street, New York, NY 10010.

If an agent takes you on as an author, the responsibility for submitting your manuscript to publishers will be out of your hands. Of course, the feedback will also be out of your hands, though some agents will send you publishers' replies. Typically, if an agent sells an author's work, the agent receives from ten to fifteen percent of the total advance and royalties.

Whether you send your writing to an agent or a publisher, it is usually not a good idea to submit to more than one at a time. If you plan to send multiple submissions, inform the agents or editors. *Never* send a photocopy of your cover letter. Agents or editors who see a photocopied cover letter will assume that the writer didn't care to make the effort to write an individual letter—and they'll be right.

Magazine and newspaper publishing differs from book publishing. Decisions are made more quickly—editors work with a lead time of hours, days, or weeks rather than months or even years. Still, you should send your work to a particular editor, and you should send a query first. Whether you are trying to publish a short story, a news article, or a magazine article, the same rules for querying editors hold true:

1. Limit yourself to one page. In that page, introduce yourself and your past experience as a writer. If you have no past experience, don't mention it.
2. Tell the editor why you are the best writer for the job. For example, you want to write an article on the yearly bamboo festival in your town because your ancestors were the first to bring bamboo to the area. Or the article on the devastating

effects of the 1993 flood in the Midwest should be yours because you were there—as a volunteer, you worked in flood relief for three months.

3. Outline the structure of your article or story briefly. Include a few facts or anecdotes. Whet your editor's appetite. Also, tell the editor the intended length of your manuscript. In magazine and newspaper publishing, length is important.

THE MARKETS

If you are turned down by agents (and many of them are completely overloaded with authors) you can try submitting to publishers yourself. The same advice about submitting a query letter, with sample chapter or proposal, holds true for publishers too. Most publishers have a huge pile of unsolicited manuscripts (the "slush pile") that may rest for up to a year on an office shelf before they are read. If a publisher asks to see your manuscript, however, a response will be much quicker and probably more detailed. Before you send your query, get the name of an editor to whom you can address it. You can do this by calling the offices and asking the receptionist for the name of a fiction or nonfiction editor, or you can get the name from a recent edition of *Literary Marketplace,* another R. R. Bowker publication.

Some of the best-known publishers are:

Avon Books, 1350 Avenue of the Americas, New York, NY 10019.

Bantam Doubleday Dell, 1540 Broadway, New York, NY 10036.

HarperCollins Publishers, 10 East 53rd Street, New York, NY 10022.

Houghton Mifflin Co., 2 Park Street, Boston, MA 02108.

Macmillan Publishing Co., 866 Third Avenue, New York, NY 10022.

William Morrow & Co., 1350 Avenue of the Americas, New York, NY 10019.

Penguin USA, 375 Hudson Street, New York, NY 10014.

Random House, 201 East 50th Street, New York, NY 10022.

Warner Books, 1270 Avenue of the Americas, New York, NY 10020.

There are literally hundreds more, including many small and specialized presses that might be more suitable for what you have written. Use *Literary Marketplace,* which also lists publishers by subject specialization, to help you locate publishers.

If you have written a play or screenplay, your publishing needs will be different. Many companies publish and produce plays at the same time. Others simply publish them. Some of these companies are:

Baker's Play Publishing Co., 100 Chauncey Street, Boston, MA 02111.

Contemporary Drama Series, P.O. Box 7710, Colorado Springs, CO 80933.

The Dramatic Publishing Co., 311 Washington Street, Woodstock, IL 60098.

New York Theatre Workshop, 220 West 42nd Street, New York, NY 10036.

Player's Press Inc., P.O. Box 1132, Studio City, CA 91614.

For screenplays, contact:

Allied Artists, Suite 377, 859 North Hollywood Way, Burbank, CA 91505.

Unifilms Inc., 22931 Sycamore Creek Drive, Valencia, CA 91354.

If you've written a short story, your best bet for publication is probably a magazine. Some magazines that run short stories include:

The Atlantic, 745 Boylston Street, Boston, MA 02116.
Esquire, 1790 Broadway, New York, NY 10019.
Harper's Magazine, 666 Broadway, New York, NY 10012.
Ladies Home Journal, 100 Park Avenue, New York, NY 10017.
Mademoiselle, 350 Madison Avenue, New York, NY 10017.
Mother Jones, 1663 Mission Street, San Francisco, CA 94103.
The New Yorker, 20 West 43rd Street, New York, NY 10036.
Redbook, 224 West 57th Street, New York, NY 10019.

You can find other magazines that specialize in fiction listed in *Literary Marketplace.*

Perhaps you've written a news article or have an idea for a column or for a newsworthy story. Most large newspapers have special Sunday sections that include in-depth stories. Some of these are:

The Boston Globe Magazine, 135 Morrissey Boulevard, Boston, MA 02107.
The Chicago Tribune Magazine, 435 North Michigan Avenue, Chicago, IL 60611.
The Detroit Free Press Magazine, 321 West Lafayette Boulevard, Detroit, MI 48226.
The Los Angeles Times Magazine, Times Mirror Square, Los Angeles, CA 90053.
Newsday, 2 Park Avenue, New York, NY 10016.
Parade, 750 Third Avenue, New York, NY 10017.

You can address your idea for a column or your news article to a news syndicate, which sells news stories to newspapers all over the country.

Associated Press, 50 Rockefeller Plaza, New York, NY 10020.
Feature News Service, 2330 South Brentwood Boulevard, St. Louis, MO 63144.
Los Angeles Times Syndicate, Times Mirror Square, Los Angeles, CA 90053.

United Press International, 1400 I Street NW, Suite 800, Washington, DC 20005.

There are literally thousands of magazines that buy articles on subjects ranging from computer sex to camping in recreational vehicles. These magazines are listed in *Literary Marketplace* and in several directories included in the Resources section at the end of this book. If you are new to professional writing, you may wish to start with a query to a local or regional magazine. These small magazines often publish articles of local interest, so if you know something about your area that you feel might interest readers, you already have a topic for an article. Once you've published a few times in small magazines, you can begin to range farther afield.

Now you can sit back with a sigh of relief and let your writing do the work. You've polished it up in a writer's group, shared it in a workshop, found yourself an agent, located a publisher. There's nothing more to do . . . except get to work on your next piece. Good luck!

VII

Resources

Resources

If you want additional information on anything discussed in this book, the resources listed here can help you.

PART I

Bovee, Courtland. *Business Communication Today.* New York: McGraw-Hill, 1991.

Collier, Oscar. *How to Write and Sell Your First Nonfiction Book.* New York: St. Martins Press, 1990.

Forman, J. *The Random House Guide to Business Writing.* New York: McGraw-Hill, 1990.

Fredette, Jean, ed. *Writer's Digest Handbook of Magazine Article Writing.* Cincinnati, OH: Writer's Digest, 1990.

Frome, Shelly. *Playwriting: A Complete Guide to Creating Theater.* Jefferson, NC: McFarland & Co., 1990.

Johnson, Dan. *Creative Guide to Journal Writing.* Louisville, CO: Gateway Publishers, 1989.

Jolliffe, David. *Advances in Writing Research.* Norwood, NJ: Ablex Publishers, 1988.

Mandell, Judy, ed. *Fiction Writer's Guidelines.* Jefferson, NC: McFarland & Co., 1988.

McKeown, Tom. *Powerful Business Writing.* Cincinnati, OH: Writer's Digest, 1992.

Robinson, Eleanor. *Concise Guide to Writing Research Papers*. Lockport, NY: E.M. Robinson, 1984.

Rubenstein, Paul. *Writing for the Media*. Englewood Cliffs, NJ: Prentice Hall, 1988.

Tarshis, Barry. *How to Write Like a Pro: A Guide to Effective Nonfiction Writing*. New York: New American Library, 1982.

Wolff, Jurgen. *Successful Scriptwriting*. Cincinnati, OH: Writer's Digest, 1991.

Woods, Bruce, ed. *Writer's Yearbook*. Cincinnati, OH: R & W Publications, Inc., 1991.

PART II

Burack, Sylvia. *The Writer's Handbook 1993*. Boston, MA: The Writer Inc. Publishers, 1993.

Donald, E. *Writing Clear Sentences*. Englewood Cliffs, NJ: Prentice Hall, 1987.

Donald, Robert. *Writing Clear Paragraphs*. Englewood Cliffs, NJ: Prentice Hall, 1987.

Fowler, Henry. *Dictionary of Modern English Usage*. New York: Oxford University Press, 1965.

Lester, James. *A Writer's Handbook: Style and Grammar*. Orlando, FL: Harcourt Brace, 1990.

Porosky, Peter. *How to Find Your Own Voice*. Lanham, MD: University Press of America, 1986.

Princeton Language Institute, ed. *21st Century Grammar Handbook*. New York: Dell Publishing, 1993.

_____. *21st Century Manual of Style*. New York: Dell Publishing, 1993.

Strunk, William, and White, E.B. *Elements of Style*. New York: Macmillan, Inc., 1979.

PART III

Chicago Manual of Style. 13th ed., Chicago, IL: University of Chicago Press, 1982.

Ehrlich, Eugene. *Schaum's Outline of Punctuation, Capitalization, and Spelling*. New York: McGraw-Hill, 1991.

Lauther, Howard. *Punctuation Thesaurus of the American Language*. Boston, MA: Branden Publishing Co., 1991.

Princeton Language Institute, ed. *21st Century Guide to Acronyms and Abbreviations*. New York: Dell Publishing, 1993.

____. *21st Century Misspeller's Dictionary*. New York: Dell Publishing, 1993.

____. *21st Century Spelling Dictionary*. New York: Dell Publishing, 1993.

Strumpf, Michael. *Webster's New World Guide to Punctuation*. New York: Simon & Schuster, 1988.

PART IV

ALA World Encyclopedia of Library and Information Services. Chicago, IL: ALA Publishing Services, 1986.

American Reference Books Annual. Englewood, CO: Libraries Unlimited, 1992.

Anderson, Laura. *Handbook for Proofreading*. Lincolnwood, IL: NTC Publishing Corp., 1990.

De Maggio, Janice, ed. *Directory of Special Libraries and Information Centers*. Detroit, MI: Gale Research Co., 1993.

Mundis, Jerrold. *Break Writer's Block Now*. New York: St. Martins Press, 1991.

Neff, Glenda, ed. *The Writer's Essential Desk Reference*. Cincinnati, OH: Writer's Digest, 1991.

Princeton Language Institute, ed. *Roget's 21st Century Thesaurus*. New York: Dell Publishing, 1993.

Sharpe, Leslie T., and Irene Gunther. *Editing Fact and Fiction: A Concise Guide to Book Editing*. New York: Cambridge University Press, 1994.

PART V

Consumer Guide Computer Buying Guide. Lincolnwood, IL: Publications International, Ltd., 1991.

Koen, William. *Fine Lines: Planning, Drafting, and Revising on the Computer*. Boston, MA: Houghton Mifflin Co., 1992.

Marcaccio, Kathleen, ed. *Directory of Online Databases*. Detroit, MI: Gale Research Co., 1993.

Princeton Language Institute, ed. *21st Century Dictionary of Computer Terms*. New York: Dell Publishing, 1994.

Sileo, Lorraine, ed. *Online Services*. Wilton, CT: Simba Information Inc., 1992.

ADDRESSES OF DATABASE SERVICES

CompuServe
5000 Arlington Centre Boulevard
P.O. Box 20212
Columbus, OH 43220

America Online
8619 Westwood Center Drive
Vienna, VA 22182

Prodigy
P.O. Box 191486
Dallas, TX 75219

Genie
P.O. Box 6403
Rockville, MD 20850

DIALOG Information Retrieval Service
3460 Hillview Avenue
Palo Alto, CA 94304

PART VI

Books and Magazines: A Guide to Publishing and Bookselling Courses in the United States. Princeton, NJ: Peterson's Guides, 1991.

Directory of Small Magazines, Presses, Editors, and Publishers. Paradise, CA: Dustbooks, 1993.

Fulton, Len, ed. *International Directory of Little Magazines and Small Presses.* Paradise, CA: Dustbooks, 1992.

Gates, Leslie. *Scriptwriter's Market.* Hollywood, CA: Script Writers, 1988.

Insider's Guide to Book Editors, Publishers, and Literary Agents. Rocklin, CA: Prima Publishing, 1992.

Kaplan, Dorlene, ed. *The Guide to Writer's Conferences.* Coral Gables, FL: Shawguides, Inc., 1992.

Kissling, Mark, ed. *Writer's Market.* Cincinnati, OH: Writer's Digest, 1993.

Literary Marketplace. New York: R.R. Bowker, 1994.

The 1994–1995 Directory of Literary Magazines. New York: Council of Literary Magazines and Presses, 1994.

Veatch, Nancy, ed. *Working Press of the Nation.* Chicago, IL: National Research Bureau, 1992.

The Laurel logo stands for the finest in contemporary fiction and nonfiction